For Dennis Prescott, cooking is all about connection—sharing great food with those you love. *Cook with Confidence* encourages you to do just that, loaded with recipes guaranteed to satisfy and acce͟͟͟ your cooking. Pa guides you step-b cooking quandary making fresh past͟͟͟osing sustainable fish, or mastering the grill.

Inside you'll find recipes that are impressive as they are approachable, inspired by Dennis's travels, his work in professional kitchens, and his Maritime roots. There's no shortage of scrumptious options, starting with snacks and starters for every occasion like Carrot and Coriander Fritters with Turmeric Yogurt. Add a seasonal salad or succulent side by serving Roasted Squash and Heirloom Tomato Panzanella or Zucchini, Blue Cheese, and Leek Gratin. Enjoy plant-powered, mouth-watering mains like Falafel Mezze Bowls or Mushroom Ragù with Cheesy Grits. While showstopping fish and meat dishes include Grilled Halibut Tacos with Creamy Slaw and Avocado Crema, and Steak Frites with Creamy Whiskey Peppercorn Sauce.

Dennis invites cooks of all levels to approach each recipe through his eyes: as your next great adventure. Exploring dishes that hone important kitchen skills and impart crucial cooking wisdom, *Cook with Confidence* inspires readers to get excited about cooking—and to create community and conversation over irresistible food.

COOK WITH CONFIDENCE

Over 100 Inspiring
Recipes to Cook and Eat Together

Dennis Prescott

Published by Harper Celebrate, an imprint of HarperCollins Focus LLC.

Cover and interior design by Terri Nimmo
Food photography, food styling, and prop styling by Dennis Prescott
Lifestyle photography by Al Douglas
Cover photo by Al Douglas

Any internet addresses (websites, blogs, etc.) in this book are offered as a resource. They are not intended in any way to be or imply an endorsement by HarperCollins Focus LLC, nor does HarperCollins Focus LLC vouch for the content of these sites for the life of this book.

ISBN 978-1-4002-5106-3 (HC)
ISBN 978-1-4002-5116-2 (epub)

Printed in Malaysia

24 25 26 27 28 COS 5 4 3 2 1

To food,
community,
and the
power of eating
together.

Contents

Introduction

I didn't start cooking until I was an adult—like, a full-on, questionably-responsible-with-a-cell-phone-bill adult. I grew up as a Led Zeppelin–obsessed kid in the magically beautiful coastal Canadian province of New Brunswick, raised in the small but mighty town of Riverview. The home of all things seafood, the highest tides on Earth, and some of the best people you could imagine, it was an incredible place to grow up and a beautiful life. I did not dream of becoming a chef, never thought I'd write one cookbook, let alone two, and surely didn't imagine I'd be the host of a food-focused television show. Mind-blowing. Instead, I had my sights set on a very different dream—becoming a full-time musician.

I vividly remember my dad coming home after a successful Saturday morning spent solo yard-saling with a vintage, slightly beaten up, incredible short-scale acoustic guitar for me. Eleven-year-old Dennis was . . . in heaven. I sat in my room for hours, learning every early nineties grunge or punk riff I could poorly pull off. With Pearl Jam posters on my wall and Smells Like Teen Spirit as my anthem, I was immediately obsessed. It was an obsession that would last almost twenty years.

After dropping out of business school (sorry, Mom and Dad) and working every odd job—from landscaping at a golf course to the late-night shift stacking toilet paper packages onto pallets—the musician's life I had dreamed of started very slowly to manifest. Our band began to get some local traction. We played shows. Lots of shows. We made our first record, crossing the Atlantic to work at the legendary Abbey Road Studios. We bought a questionably reliable van and started touring the country. It was hard. It was perfect. It was nirvana, I loved it, every single second.

Part of the deal when you're a full-time traveling musician is that you spend basically 365 days a year crammed into a fifteen-passenger van on the road. You meet loads of people, make countless fifteen-minute friends, you play a lot of venues, you arrive home—to a motel room or a friend's couch or, occasionally, your actual home—and you eat some crummy food, and then you do it again. And again. The other part is that the musician's life is rich in experience . . . only. I was broke and living dollar to dollar. During those years, the microwave, late-night dollar menus, and PB&Js were my best friends. Like, I really knew my way around a microwave.

After years of touring as musicians, crisscrossing North America and playing in just about every venue from Lewisporte to Burnaby, our band of misfits sold almost everything we owned, packed up our essentials, and on a whim, a prayer, and a few dollars (I mean, a few), relocated south of the Mason Dixon to sunny Music City. A last kick at the can to see if we had what it takes to make it in the music industry (whatever that means). It was by far the most creatively inspiring, emotionally stretching, and all-together life-changing time I'd ever experienced.

I loved the travel. I loved the reckless adventure. I loved being in the studio. But the lifestyle was . . . challenging. Our apartment choices were dodgy at best. I slept on an air mattress for almost two years, with the lights on to keep the cockroaches at bay. Lack of funds and any knowledge of how to make my way around the kitchen led to me being really out of shape, not taking care of my physical or mental health, and being in dire need of a change. I was struggling, and I needed help. I knew that if I wanted to take control of my health, part of that meant I needed to learn how to cook. I loved food. I'd experienced life-changing moments at the table, tasting new and exciting dishes on the road, and wanted to be able to re-create those experiences myself and with my crew at home. At the time, YouTube didn't really exist, food-based blogs were still a very new resource, and I, of course, couldn't afford to take any cooking lessons or go back to school. At the suggestion of a bandmate, I visited the Nashville Public Library and borrowed three cookbooks. What seemed a simple act at the time would go on to literally change my life forever.

I remember that inaugural dish I cooked like it was yesterday. It's imprinted in my mind. I made a chicken korma recipe from a Jamie Oliver book (thanks, Jamie), re-creating a dish I'd experienced while recording in the UK years before, and gathered all of my band and studio mates to our Brentwood apartment. We joined three smaller tables as one and sat in camping chairs (you know, the ones with cup holders built into the armrests). There's a beautiful moment of hush that comes over the table when everyone tucks in for their first bite. It gets quiet, like putting noise canceling headphones on, just for a second. Then it gradually gets louder and louder, those first few bites of deliciousness ushering in an incredible chorus of community, laughter, and fun at the table. That's the very moment I fell in love with cooking. It hit me like a ton of bricks. I fell in love with feeding people and creating beautiful memories at the table. It was the moment I realized I could create emotional, nostalgic, forever-type memories at the table, just like I'd experienced performing on stage and playing someone's favorite song.

I'd love to tell you I was a cooking wunderkind, but it would be a lie. The learning curve was steep; I failed a lot. But I failed forward. I became almost obsessively curious. Over the next couple of years, I lived in the kitchen. I cooked all day, every day, creating everything from scratch and learning the method, the madness, and the history of each and every dish. I also started taking care of my physical health and began running. A minute run, then a minute walk at first and gradually working my way up from there. After one year of cooking constantly, I went from crawling to walking in the kitchen, and I went from walking to running on the hard pavement. I lost almost ninety pounds. I felt incredible, like I gained a new lease on life, and I'd found a new passion. I had zero thought of this culinary pursuit becoming a career; I just loved cooking and gathering folks at the table.

Over the next few years, I fumbled my way in a couple restaurants, catered in the Hamptons, ran a coffee and doughnut market pop-up, and cooked my ass off, ever learning. I started an Instagram account, wrote a column for *Food & Wine* magazine, worked with countless brands, wrote a bestselling cookbook, started to do TV, found a wood-fired passion with Traeger Grills, and traveled the globe as an ambassador with World Vision and Chef's Manifesto. What may have seemed to some to have happened overnight was a very slow and steady burn. I'm forever grateful for every gift this beautiful life has afforded me. But no matter the experience, for me, it always came back to my community and the communal table.

A chef's life has become glamorous as of late. The reality is that being a cook, whether in a restaurant or a home kitchen, is an act of service. We serve. And it's an honor to serve. It's not glamorous, often much more the opposite. It's hard, it's dirty, it's intense, and it's the most rewarding thing I've had the joy of committing my life to. I fell in love with feeding people, with a crowded table, with the sense of community that comes from cooking and eating together. I fell in love with the possibility and promise of the table. It's where we connect, where we invest in one another, where we grow closer. If my friends provided a wonderful test case for this, it was only when I began traveling a lot for work that I really realized how true it is. I've been fortunate to traverse the globe, and everywhere I go, food is the ambassador and the table is the board room. It doesn't matter what language we speak or where we come from, we all have a favorite food, and we all love celebrating together with loved ones at the table. Food can and often is the great equalizer, the master connector. Community begins at the table over plates of some of my favorites, like cacio e pepe (page 88), bowlfuls of rich fish chowder (page 150), or platters of chicken teriyaki (page 195).

The recipes in this book reflect this past decade of travel and my Maritime childhood. As a kid growing up in Canada, there were a lot of ingredients I didn't have access to and a lot I hadn't tasted. But my travels opened me up—they expanded my heart and my palate and changed me as a cook. An explosion of flavor! I experienced life-changing dishes that completely reshaped my culinary journey. And I absolutely love the fact that we get to travel the globe through dishes we create in our home kitchens. I couldn't write a cookbook today without acknowledging all I've learned along the way—many of the recipes in this cookbook certainly weren't things I grew up eating, but they've found a place in my life and diet and are so exciting and wonderful I've no doubt they'll find a home in yours too.

This book is filled with rock-solid keeper recipes for every occasion, the kind you can turn to again and again. That means everything from quick snacks and starters, ranging from a simple ceviche (page 17) to fully loaded nachos (page 21); lightning-fast weeknight hits, like Sriracha Maple Salmon with Avocado Pineapple Salsa (page 169) or Mint and Aleppo Pepper Chicken Kebabs (page 209); giant dinner salads, including my riff on a Nicoise salad topped with blackened trout (page 51); and special occasion recipes for when you want to pull out all the stops, like Steak Frites with Creamy Whiskey Peppercorn Sauce (page 245) or grilled lobsters with compound butter (page 181).

But beyond the recipes, this book will help you become a better cook, whether you're just getting started or are seasoned in the kitchen (pun intended; sorry). I've filled its pages with all the cooking lessons that I've learned along the way, things like how to open an oyster, how to choose the best seafood, how to become a total grill master, how to make pasta from scratch, and how to stock your pantry with an array of ingredients, including some of my favorites like miso, smoked paprika, and fresh citrus, that will punch up the flavor of anything you cook. This book is intended as a resource for cooks at all levels, with recipes that will reinforce the lessons in the most delicious way possible.

But, really, my fervent hope is that the recipes in this book inspire you to cook for your people, to spend more time at the communal table, and that in doing so you're able to experience the boundless joy that comes from it. No matter where you find yourself in the culinary journey, I hope you find inspiration and happiness in cooking from these pages.

Kick start My Heart

Snacks and Starters for Every Delicious Occasion

This might be the part of the evening I anticipate most. It's magic. The ultimate buzz. My crew has arrived, and there's the excitement of being together, hugs, high-fives, everyone talking over everyone else (classic). Vibe city. Music is bumping. Somebody's brought a six-pack, or a bottle of wine, someone else has arrived with a bouquet (lovely of them) I hastily stick into a vase. Everyone arrives hungry, ready to catch up over dinner or the game, and mostly, just pumped to be together as one big family. Food is community. Community is everything.

And of course, there's always deliciousness to eat. Always. It could be something simple, like a big bowl of cheesy baked crab and shrimp dip or chicken wings hot off the grill, tossed with a salty, sticky-sweet pineapple glaze. Other times, I offer something more substantial, like fully loaded nachos or fried zucchini blossoms filled with lemony ricotta, depending on the mood and what's in season at the market.

The purpose of the snacks in this chapter is to whet, not sate, the appetite, and accordingly, they're meant to be shared. If you have a bigger crowd, make a few of these recipes and serve them together to kick off a meal, or as a meal unto themselves, any time of day (or night).

Oysters on the Half Shell with Kimchi Cocktail Sauce and Limoncello-Chili Granita

For the granita

½ cup coconut sugar

1 bird's eye or Thai chili, stemmed and very finely chopped

½ cup limoncello

¼ cup freshly squeezed lemon juice

Zest of 1 lemon

For the cocktail sauce

½ cup Heinz-style chili sauce

½ cup ketchup

2 tablespoons freshly squeezed lemon juice

1 tablespoon prepared horseradish

2 tablespoons finely chopped prepared kimchi

1 dash Worcestershire sauce

1 dash Tabasco

Sea salt and freshly ground black pepper

2 dozen of your favorite oysters, on the half shell (see page 13)

Oysters are one of the best ways to truly experience merroir, or "taste of place." Every oyster is unique, its flavor highly affected by the water where it was grown. Atlantic, Pacific, north, and south—oysters from each region are distinctive. I'll forever be biased toward the briny and sweet oysters grown up and down the New Brunswick Acadian Shores, but one of my favorite things is trying new and exciting varietals as I travel to different seaside regions around the globe.

When I serve them raw, on the half shell, I always make different toppings to serve alongside. My kimchi cocktail sauce is like a classic cocktail sauce but with chili sauce in addition to ketchup. And the limoncello-chili granita—made with the ultra-citrusy Italian liqueur—both flavors the oysters and keeps them ice cold (which you definitely want when serving raw oysters).

Make the Granita: Combine 2 cups water and the sugar in a small saucepan, and bring to a gentle simmer over medium heat. Simmer for 5 minutes. When the sugar has dissolved entirely, remove from the heat, and add the chili. Let stand for 30 minutes, and then pass through a fine-mesh sieve set over a medium bowl. Stir in the limoncello, lemon juice, and lemon zest, and transfer to an 8 x 8-inch freezer-safe baking dish. Freeze, scraping and mixing with a fork every 30 to 45 minutes, until completely frozen into icy crystals (about 3 to 4 hours).

Make the Cocktail Sauce: Combine the chili sauce, ketchup, lemon juice, horseradish, kimchi, Worcestershire sauce, and Tabasco in a medium bowl and mix well. Season to taste with salt and pepper. I prefer to leave my cocktail as is, but if you prefer a smoother sauce, pulse with a hand blender until smooth.

Fill a platter or rimmed baking sheet with coarse salt or crushed ice to help stabilize the oysters. Set the oysters on the prepared platter. Scoop the granita into a bowl and serve it and the seafood sauce alongside.

This recipe makes more of the sauce and the granita than you'll need (it's a good problem to have), and both will keep for a second round of oysters. Store the kimchi cocktail sauce in an airtight container in the refrigerator for up to 2 weeks. Store the leftover granita in a freezer-safe container with a lid in the freezer for up to 2 weeks. Fluff with a fork before serving.

How to Open an Oyster

Oysters are among the most sustainable shellfish we can consume. Because they're a saltwater bivalve mollusk, they're brilliant at filtering dirty seawater (adult oysters can filter up to fifty-five quarts of water a day). They play a vital role in keeping seawater balanced so other species can thrive. Their shells capture carbon dioxide. They extract nitrogen from waterways. They form natural reefs when they grow in the wild. Oysters. Are. Incredible.

Whether your oysters are from the East, West, or Gulf coast, the method for opening them is the same. To begin, fold a clean kitchen towel lengthwise into thirds. This helps prevent the wet oyster from slipping. An oyster knife is a short dull knife well suited to the task; while you might be tempted to substitute something else (your nice paring knife, a screwdriver), resist the urge and get the right tool for the job.

Oysters are cup shaped; one shell is relatively flat, while the other is rounded. Set the oyster rounded side down on the folded towel. If you're right-handed, position the oyster so that its hinge (where the shells connect) is pointing to the right; if you're a lefty, you'll want to point that hinge to the left. Fold the towel over the oyster so that only the hinge is exposed, and place your nondominant hand on top to hold it steady. Try to bunch up the folded towel in front of that hand so that if the oyster knife slips, the towel will protect you.

Work your oyster knife into the hinge. This is not an exercise in brute force; rather, you're just trying to find the spot around the hinge area where you can get enough of the tip of the oyster knife between the shells to give you some leverage. Once you feel like you've got the knife tip solidly in place, wiggle the oyster knife up and down while also twisting and rotating it and applying gentle pressure until the shell pops apart a tiny bit. Continue to twist your knife so that the flat part of the blade prizes the shells apart even more. Inside the oyster, a muscle connects the top and bottom shell, which needs to be severed to open the oyster completely. To do this, start from the hinge end and slide the flat of the oyster knife blade across the oyster, trying to keep the knife as flat as possible so you don't slice into the oyster itself. Once you cut the muscle, you should be able to pull the top shell off. Use the knife to gently free any oyster meat that is still clinging to the top shell.

Discard the top shell, and examine the oyster for any bits of shell that might have gotten in when you opened it (a gritty oyster is an unpleasant oyster). Use the clean tip of your oyster knife to discard them. Then slide your oyster knife under the oyster, severing the muscle that connects it to the bottom shell. The oyster is now ready to eat. If you'll be enjoying these on the half shell, transfer to a rimmed dish filled with crushed ice or salt, which will help stabilize the oysters so they don't tip and spill all the juices. If using in another recipe (such as a chowder), simply tip the oyster and its juices into a bowl, and discard the bottom shell.

Baked Oysters with Garlic Butter and Parmesan Pangrattato

For the pangrattato

2 tablespoons extra-virgin olive oil

2 tablespoons salted butter

½ cup panko breadcrumbs

1 garlic clove, minced

Zest of ½ lemon

2 tablespoons chopped fresh flat-leaf parsley, plus more for garnish

Sea salt and freshly ground black pepper

½ cup grated Parmesan cheese

For the compound butter

½ cup (1 stick) salted butter, softened

2 teaspoons minced fresh flat-leaf parsley

2 teaspoons minced fresh basil

1 garlic clove, minced

1½ teaspoons lemon zest

½ teaspoon dried crushed red pepper flakes

¼ teaspoon each sea salt and freshly ground black pepper

2 dozen of your favorite oysters, on the half shell (see page 13)

If I'm not crushing them by the dozen on the half shell, my other favorite way of preparing oysters is baking them. Golden-baked perfection. Here, the briny bivalves are lavished with a glorious garlicky herbed compound butter, spiced up with red pepper flakes, and then topped with crunchy breadcrumbs. Basically, heaven in a bite. You'll have extra compound butter; you can toss it with vegetables, throw it on a baked potato, spoon it over a seared steak, or wrap it tightly and put it in the freezer for another round of oysters. And if you're serving these as a grill-night starter, be sure to bake these on your grill for that extra depth of smoky flavor.

Preheat the oven (or grill) to 400°F and line a rimmed baking sheet with parchment paper.

Make the Pangrattato: Heat the olive oil and butter in a large skillet over medium heat. When the butter has melted, add the panko, garlic, lemon zest, and parsley, and season with a good pinch of salt and pepper. Cook, stirring often, until the panko is crispy and light golden brown, about 3 to 4 minutes. Remove from the heat, fold in the Parmesan, and mix well. Set aside.

Make the Compound Butter: In a medium bowl, combine the butter, parsley, basil, garlic, lemon zest, red pepper flakes, salt, and pepper, and mix well until completely combined and smooth.

Arrange the oysters in a single layer on the prepared baking sheet. Top each oyster with about 1 teaspoon of compound butter, and sprinkle over a generous portion of the pangrattato. Transfer to the oven and bake for about 8 to 10 minutes, until the oysters are cooked through and the topping is perfectly golden brown. Serve immediately.

Store any leftover compound butter in an airtight container in the refrigerator for up to 2 days or in the freezer for up to 2 months. Add a pat of it to a piece of seared fish or steak, toss it with pasta, or use it to dress simple steamed or roasted vegetables.

Coconut Habanero Whitefish Ceviche

Juice of 4 large lemons

Juice of 6 limes

Juice of 1 large orange

½ cup canned unsweetened full-fat coconut milk

2 tablespoons mild-flavored honey

1½ teaspoons minced fresh ginger

1 garlic clove, minced

½ large red onion, finely chopped

1 habanero pepper, seeded and minced (or less, depending on how spicy you like it)

Sea salt

1½ pounds boneless white fish fillets, skinned and cubed into ¼-inch cubes (I like snapper, halibut, or sea bass)

1 large ripe mango, peeled and diced

1 large plum tomato, cored, seeded, and finely chopped

¼ cup minced fresh cilantro

A big bowl of tortilla chips, for serving

I absolutely adore ceviche. It's light and refreshing, entirely customizable, and a perfect dish for those warm summer evenings when you're craving something delicious, but it's too hot to turn on the stove. I originally created this dish for my friends Fluffy and Sue in palm-treed and sunshine-kissed Saint Lucia. That original dish was prepared with lionfish, an invasive (but delicious) species in the region, in hopes that more folks would enjoy the fish on a daily basis and, as a by-product, help with the sustainability of our marine ecosystem.

Ceviche is raw fish that is marinated or "cooked" in citrus. Of course, because it is still technically raw, you want to source the best-quality, sashimi-grade fish available in your area and mix it with the citrus just before serving so it doesn't "overcook" and turn rubbery. For this preparation, I like to use a mild white fish, such as snapper or halibut, but you should choose whatever looks freshest and best at your local market.

Pour the lemon, lime, and orange juices into a large bowl. Stir in the coconut milk and honey, and then add the ginger, garlic, onion, habanero, and season with salt. Mix well and then taste and adjust the seasoning as necessary (adding a little more salt or a little more honey—balance is key).

Place the fish in the bowl and give everything a mix, making sure that each piece of fish has been kissed by citrus juice. Cover with plastic wrap and chill in the fridge for 30 minutes or up to 1 hour, if you prefer the fish a little more "cooked through." As the fish sits, the acid from the citrus juices will denature the proteins in the fish, firming up the flesh and giving it a cooked texture.

Just before serving, stir in the mango, tomato, and cilantro, taste, and season with salt. Serve with tortilla chips for scooping.

Clam and Fennel Bruschetta

5 pounds littleneck clams

¼ cup extra-virgin olive oil, plus more for drizzling

1 medium onion, thinly sliced

1 medium fennel bulb, thinly sliced, fronds reserved

Sea salt

4 garlic cloves, minced

½ teaspoon crushed red pepper flakes

2 tablespoons chopped fresh tarragon

¼ cup dry white wine

2 large Roma tomatoes, diced

2 tablespoons freshly squeezed lemon juice

2 tablespoons chopped fresh flat-leaf parsley

2 tablespoons chopped fresh chives

Freshly ground black pepper

12 thick-cut slices of your favorite sourdough bread, toasted

1 lemon cut into wedges, for serving

This summer-friendly snack is inspired by a beachside dish I enjoyed at a little restaurant on the Italian coast. There they used vongole, tiny little clams, each hardly bigger than my thumbnail. Because they're not readily available here, I use littleneck clams, which are a perfectly fine substitute. Up and down the Acadian Shores, folks can clams every year (known as palourdes en bouteille) for use during the cold, harsh New Brunswick winters. If you want, you could substitute best-quality canned clams during the off-season, as Maritimers often do.

Rinse the clams well to remove any dirt or sand. Place in a bowl and add cold water to cover. Let stand for 20 minutes (this brief soak will cause the clams to expel any sand that may be trapped in the shell). Remove and discard any clams that are open or have broken shells. Bring 1 cup of water to a boil in a large pot. Add the clams, cover, and cook for 5 to 10 minutes, until the clams open (discard any clams that do not open). Pull the clam meat from each shell and place in a bowl; discard the shells. Pour any juices from the pot through a fine-mesh strainer into a medium bowl.

Heat the olive oil in a large skillet over medium heat until the oil is shimmering. Carefully add the onion and fennel, season with a pinch of salt, and cook until the vegetables are softened, about 5 to 6 minutes. Add the garlic and red pepper flakes and cook for 30 seconds, and then pour in the white wine and reserved clam juice and bring to a simmer. Cook until the liquid is reduced by half, add the clam meat, and simmer until the clams are just warmed through, about 2 minutes.

Remove from the heat and stir in the tomatoes, lemon juice, parsley, and chives, and season to taste with salt and pepper.

Drizzle each slice of bread with a bit of oil, and pile the clam mixture onto the toasts, dividing evenly. Garnish with some fennel fronds and serve with lemon.

Loaded Grilled Chicken Nachos

For the chicken

2 pounds boneless, skinless chicken thighs

2 tablespoons extra-virgin olive oil

2 tablespoons tequila

Zest of 1 lime

2 teaspoons chili powder

1½ teaspoons smoked paprika

½ teaspoon ground cumin

¼ teaspoon ground cayenne pepper

1½ teaspoons sea salt

1 teaspoon freshly ground black pepper

For the pico de gallo

1½ pounds plum tomatoes (about 6), cored and diced

1 medium red onion, finely chopped

½ cup chopped fresh cilantro

Juice of 2 limes

1½ teaspoons extra-virgin olive oil

Sea salt

For the guacamole

3 ripe avocados, halved, seeded, and peeled

2 tablespoons freshly squeezed lime juice, plus more to taste

¼ cup finely chopped red onion

1 plum tomato, diced

1 jalapeño pepper, stemmed, seeded, and minced

1 garlic clove, minced

2 tablespoons finely chopped fresh cilantro

Sea salt

It would be impossible for me to write a chapter about snacks without including a recipe for the almighty nacho, the MVP of snack time. Growing up, my brother and I ate a lot of nachos. A lot. They competed head-to-head with ice cream as our after-school, after-sports, and late-evening addictive food of choice. Our nacho love began as equal parts chips and cheese (with some store-bought salsa), and then grew to everything and anything we could find in the fridge. Nachoing: It's a verb. It's an art.

Nachos, unquestionably, are shareable snack-time perfection. While calling nachos healthy would be a stretch, my nachos are bright and flavorful, thanks to the addition of a fresh tomato salsa and homemade guacamole. The more toppings the better, as far as I'm concerned. Grilling the chicken adds another layer of smoky flavor (if you have leftover grilled chicken, this recipe is a great way to use it up). Perfect for game night, when loads of friends come over, or any random Wednesday.

Marinate the Chicken: In a large bowl, combine the chicken thighs, olive oil, tequila, lime zest, chili powder, paprika, cumin, cayenne, salt, and pepper, and mix well. Cover and refrigerate for at least 4 hours or up to 24 hours. Let the chicken come to room temperature before grilling. Shortly before you plan to serve the nachos, prepare the toppings.

Make the Pico de Gallo: In a medium bowl, combine the tomatoes, onion, and cilantro, and mix well. Add the lime juice and olive oil, and then season with salt to taste. Set aside.

Make the Guacamole: In a medium bowl, smash the avocado into a chunky purée. Add the lime juice and stir to combine. Stir in the onion, tomato, jalapeño, garlic, cilantro, and a few pinches of salt. Taste and add more lime juice or salt as necessary. Set aside.

Prepare the Sour Cream: In a small bowl, stir together the sour cream, lime juice, chili powder, paprika, and a pinch of salt. Refrigerate until ready to serve.

Grill the Chicken: Preheat a grill for direct, high-heat grilling (see Notes on Grilling, page 187). Remove the chicken from the marinade (discard the marinade). Grill, flipping halfway through, until lightly charred and an instant-read thermometer inserted in the thickest part of the chicken reaches 165°F, about 12 to 15 minutes. Let rest for 10 minutes, and then use two forks or your fingers to shred the chicken into bite-size pieces.

Line a baking sheet with parchment paper and preheat the oven to 400°F.

ingredients and recipe continue

For the sour cream

½ cup sour cream

1 tablespoon freshly squeezed lime juice

1 teaspoon chili powder

½ teaspoon smoked paprika

Sea salt

For assembly and serving

1 large bag (about 12 ounces) tortilla chips

1 small red onion, peeled and very thinly sliced

½ red bell pepper, stemmed, seeded, and very thinly sliced

2 cups grated aged cheddar cheese

2 cups grated Monterey Jack cheese

1 jalapeño pepper, thinly sliced

1 radish, thinly sliced

¼ cup cilantro leaves

Lime wedges

Assemble the Nachos: Arrange the tortilla chips in an even layer on the baking sheet, and top with the grilled chicken, sliced onion, bell pepper, and cheddar and Jack cheeses, scattering evenly. Bake until the cheese has melted and the chips at the edge of the baking sheet are starting to brown, about 6 to 8 minutes. Remove from the oven and serve immediately with your pico de gallo, guacamole, spiked sour cream, jalapeño, radish, cilantro, and lime wedges.

Cooking Note: Technically, you're not grilling the nachos, but you can use a hot grill the same way as you might use an oven: to melt the cheese, crisp up the chips, and make everything delicious. If you want to try this method, it's simple, provided you have a grill surface that's large enough to accommodate a baking sheet. While the grill is still hot, set the baking sheet of nachos directly on the grill grate, making sure the bottom and top vents of the grill are open. Cover and cook until the cheese has melted and the chips at the edge of the baking sheet are starting to brown, about 6 to 8 minutes.

Two Party Dips

Dip is a ubiquitous party staple, so I often include one when I'm preparing snacks for a crowd. These are two of my all-time desert island favorites.

Creamed Lobster Dip

This ultra-rich dip is one of my favorite party tricks—it's a breeze to prepare, everybody absolutely loves it, and the simplicity of the dish really makes the lobster sing. Make sure the cream cheese is at room temperature, which will give you the smoothest dip. If you'd like, you can serve the dip warm—bake at 350°F for 20 minutes until bubbly and browned. Hot damn!

SERVES 4 TO 6

½ cup mayonnaise, homemade (page 118) or store-bought

½ cup cream cheese, at room temperature

1 pound cooked lobster meat, finely chopped

Zest of 1 lemon, divided

1 tablespoon freshly squeezed lemon juice

1 garlic clove, minced

1 tablespoon minced fresh chives, plus more to garnish

Sea salt and freshly ground black pepper

Potato chips, for serving

In a medium bowl, combine the mayonnaise and cream cheese and mix until silky smooth. Fold in the lobster, ¾ of your lemon zest, lemon juice, garlic, chives, salt, and pepper. Taste and adjust the seasoning as necessary. Transfer to a serving dish and garnish with extra chives, the remaining lemon zest, and a crack of black pepper. Serve right away with potato chips alongside, or cover and refrigerate for up to 1 day. Bring to room temperature before serving.

Cheesy Baked Crab and Shrimp Dip

This super-cheesy baked crab and shrimp dip is so addictive that, once you dip, you'll be hooked. Garlicky, seafood-packed, with brightness from the lemon and green onions, this dip is a guaranteed knockout.

SERVES 4 TO 6

8 ounces cream cheese, at room temperature

⅓ cup mayonnaise, homemade (page 118) or store-bought

¼ cup full-fat sour cream

1 tablespoon freshly squeezed lemon juice

1¼ cups grated aged cheddar cheese, divided

1¼ cups grated Monterey Jack cheese, divided

½ teaspoon Old Bay seasoning

1 teaspoon Worcestershire sauce

4 dashes Tabasco sauce

12 ounces cooked medium shrimp, deveined and chopped into bite-size pieces

8 ounces cooked crab meat

3 garlic cloves, minced

3 green onions, sliced

A few pinches black pepper

2 tablespoons chopped fresh basil

Crackers or crispy baguette, for serving

Preheat the oven to 375°F.

In the bowl of an electric mixer fitted with the paddle attachment (or in a medium bowl with a handheld mixer) beat together the cream cheese, mayonnaise, sour cream, lemon juice, ¾ cup each of the cheddar and Jack cheeses, the Old Bay, Worcestershire sauce, and Tabasco until smooth. Fold in the shrimp, crab, garlic, and green onions.

Transfer the dip to a shallow baking dish (1¼ quarts), and top with the remaining ½ cup each of the cheddar and Jack cheeses, and the pepper. Bake for 20 to 25 minutes or until golden and bubbling, then sprinkle over fresh basil. Serve hot, with crackers or baguette alongside.

23

Grilled Huli Huli Chicken Wings

For the chicken

1 cup light soy sauce

6 garlic cloves, minced

2-inch piece fresh ginger, peeled and minced

4 pounds chicken wings, a combination of flats and drums

For the pineapple sauce

1½ cups pineapple juice

⅓ cup light soy sauce

¼ cup honey

¼ cup gochujang

4 garlic cloves, minced

1-inch piece fresh ginger, peeled and minced

Juice of 1 lime

¼ cup chicken stock

¼ cup rice vinegar

For serving

1 bunch green onions, thinly sliced

1½ teaspoons toasted sesame seeds

1 cup fresh cilantro, for garnish

Flavor-Bomb Pickles (page 215) (optional but encouraged)

Huli Huli chicken was born in 1955, when a Honolulu businessperson grilled chicken, slathered it with teriyaki sauce made according to his mother's recipe, and sold it to great acclaim. Versions of the teriyaki sauce abound—some recipes contain ketchup, others use pineapple juice (such as mine), but all contain soy sauce, ginger, and garlic. I ran headfirst into a big bowl of huli huli happiness when visiting the Big Island for the first time and knew I had to create my own version based on this incredible dish. I add gochujang—a Korean red pepper paste—which is not a traditional ingredient but adds sweet spiciness. You'll absolutely love it! I like to serve this chicken with Flavor-Bomb Pickles (page 215).

Prepare the Chicken: In a large bowl, whisk together the soy sauce, garlic, and ginger. Add the wings and toss to combine. Cover with plastic wrap and refrigerate for 4 hours (or overnight, if you have the patience).

When ready to cook, heat a grill for direct, high-heat grilling (see Notes on Grilling, page 187). Remove the wings from the marinade (discard the marinade), and place the chicken wings directly on the grill. Cook for 30 to 35 minutes, turning halfway through, until the wings are well browned and cooked through. Transfer to a large heatproof bowl.

Make the Pineapple Sauce: While the wings are cooking, combine the pineapple juice, soy sauce, honey, gochujang, garlic, ginger, lime juice, stock, and vinegar in a medium saucepan and whisk until well combined and smooth. Bring to a low simmer. Let the sauce bubble and reduce for 15 to 20 minutes, stirring occasionally to prevent scorching, until thickened, glossy, and reduced by about half.

Pour the sauce over the wings and toss to coat. Add the green onions and sesame seeds, and toss again to distribute. Transfer to a serving dish and garnish with the cilantro. Serve with Flavor-Bomb Pickles, if using.

Cooking Note: *If you'd like, you can grill pineapple rings alongside the wings. When they're soft and charred, chop the rings into bite-size pieces and toss them with the wings and sauce. Highly encouraged.*

Beef and Eggplant Fatteh

4 pita breads (8-inch rounds), cut into triangles

For the chickpeas

1 can (15 ounces) chickpeas, drained and rinsed

2 tablespoons extra-virgin olive oil

2 teaspoons chili powder

1 tablespoon lemon zest

Sea salt

For the eggplant and beef

3 tablespoons extra-virgin olive oil

1 red onion, diced

Sea salt

1 medium eggplant, cut into ½-inch cubes

2 teaspoons ground cumin

2 teaspoons ground coriander

1½ teaspoons smoked paprika

1½ teaspoons sumac (optional)

1 pound ground beef (80/20 blend)

Freshly ground black pepper

For the tahini sauce

1½ cups full-fat plain yogurt

¼ cup tahini

1 garlic clove, minced

1 tablespoon freshly squeezed lemon juice

Sea salt

For assembly

⅓ cup pine nuts, for garnish

¾ cup pomegranate seeds, for garnish

2 tablespoons fresh mint, for garnish

This Levantine dish is eaten throughout the Middle East, though its specific composition varies from place to place and cook to cook. A perfectly satisfying vegetarian version could be made with eggplant alone, but I also like this hearty version, which contains both eggplant and spiced ground beef spooned over crispy pita chips and chickpeas. A garlicky tahini sauce ties the ingredients together, and the mint, pine nut, and pomegranate seed garnishes add a beautiful crunch, freshness, and color. Sumac, a brick-red spice with a tart, lemony flavor, is a great addition. You can usually find it in well-stocked grocery or specialty stores, but if you have trouble sourcing it, omit it. This is hearty enough to be served as a main course with a salad alongside, but it also makes a killer appetizer for a crowd.

Preheat the oven to 400°F and line 2 baking sheets with parchment paper.

Arrange the pita on 1 baking sheet in an even layer and bake for 10 to 15 minutes, until just starting to crisp. Set aside; keep the oven at 400°F.

Prepare the Chickpeas: In a medium bowl, toss the chickpeas with the olive oil, chili powder, lemon zest, and a generous pinch of salt, and then spread on the second prepared baking sheet. Bake until crispy and golden brown, gently shaking the baking sheet from time to time, about 25 to 30 minutes.

Prepare the Eggplant and Beef: Heat the olive oil in a large skillet over medium heat. Carefully add the onion and a pinch of salt, and cook, stirring occasionally, until softened and translucent, about 4 to 5 minutes. Add the eggplant, season again with salt, and cook, stirring often, for about 8 to 10 minutes, until the eggplant is nicely caramelized all over. Add the cumin, coriander, paprika, sumac (if using), and the beef. Season with salt and cook, breaking the beef apart using a wooden spoon, until the beef is cooked through and beginning to crisp and the eggplant is very soft, about 10 minutes. Season to taste with pepper and remove from the heat.

Make the Tahini Sauce: In a medium bowl, combine the yogurt, tahini, garlic, and lemon juice. Season with a pinch of salt. Taste and adjust the seasoning as necessary, and then set aside.

Heat a skillet over medium-low heat and add the pine nuts. Toast, stirring occasionally, until the pine nuts are golden brown and smell beautifully nutty. Remove and set aside.

Assemble the Fatteh: Arrange the pita in a single layer on a large serving platter, and top with the eggplant and beef mixture and the chickpeas. Dollop with the tahini sauce and garnish with the toasted pine nuts, pomegranate seeds, and mint.

Ricotta-Stuffed Zucchini Flowers with Marinara

For the marinara

¼ cup extra-virgin olive oil

½ teaspoon red pepper flakes

4 garlic cloves, minced

1 tablespoon tomato paste

1 can (28 ounces) crushed tomatoes

½ cup vegetable stock

1 tablespoon lemon zest

Sea salt and freshly ground black pepper

¼ cup grated Parmesan cheese

For the filling

¾ cup ricotta cheese

2½ tablespoons finely grated Parmesan cheese

Zest of 1 lemon

¼ cup finely chopped fresh basil

Sea salt and freshly ground black pepper

For the batter and frying

½ cup all-purpose flour

1 teaspoon baking powder

½ cup soda water

Sea salt

16 zucchini blossoms

Grapeseed oil or other neutral oil, for frying

Zucchini may be a ubiquitous summertime ingredient, but zucchini flowers feel special. And they *are* special. If you grow your own squash, you'll have a ready supply of flowers; otherwise, you'll be most likely to find them at the farmer's market, where seasonal deliciousness abounds! The brilliant yellow blooms are perfect purses for stuffing, and I adore a filling of lemony ricotta. Yes, they are battered and fried, but once you get the hang of it, it's really quite simple—and a wonderful, special snack for summer visitors. Serve with your favorite chilled white or macerated wine and dream of dining under the Tuscan sun.

Make the Marinara: Heat the olive oil in a medium saucepan over medium heat until the oil is shimmering. Carefully add the red pepper flakes and cook for 30 seconds. Add the garlic and cook, stirring, for 30 seconds more, keeping a close watch so that it doesn't burn. Add the tomato paste and cook for 1 minute, and then add the tomatoes, stock, and lemon zest, and season with salt and pepper. Bring to a simmer, then reduce the heat to low and let the sauce bubble away until thickened and glossy, 8 to 10 minutes. Stir in the Parmesan and remove from the heat; taste and season with salt.

Make the Filling: In a medium bowl, mix together the ricotta, Parmesan, lemon zest, and basil, and season with a good pinch of salt and pepper. Transfer the filling to a piping bag (or a resealable plastic bag with the corner cut) and refrigerate until ready to use.

Make the Batter: In a medium bowl, whisk together the flour and baking powder. Slowly pour in the soda water, while stirring constantly, until combined. Season with a pinch of salt.

Pipe about 1 to 1½ teaspoons of filling into each zucchini blossom, being careful not to overfill.

Line a baking sheet with paper towel. In a large Dutch oven or high-sided, heavy-bottomed pot, pour the grapeseed oil to a depth of 2 inches. Heat over medium heat until the oil reaches 375°F on a deep-frying thermometer. Working with a few blossoms at a time, dip the filled zucchini blossoms into the batter, turning until well coated and allowing the excess batter to drip off. Fry until golden and crispy, about 2½ to 3 minutes. Remove from the oil with a slotted spoon, transfer to the prepared baking sheet, and sprinkle with salt. Fry the rest of the blossoms in batches, letting the oil return to 375°F between each batch.

To serve, pour the marinara into a bowl and set on a platter. Arrange the blossoms around the marinara, sprinkle with sea salt, and serve immediately.

Crispy Fried Artichokes with Garlic Tarragon Sauce

For the sauce

1 head garlic

Extra-virgin olive oil, for drizzling

Sea salt and freshly ground black pepper

1 tablespoon unsalted butter

2 tablespoons all-purpose flour

1 cup whole milk

Zest of ½ lemon

1 tablespoon minced fresh tarragon

½ cup finely grated Parmesan cheese

For the artichokes

Juice of 2 lemons

3 pounds baby artichokes (about 24)

6 cups grapeseed oil or other neutral oil, for frying

Sea salt and freshly ground black pepper

¼ cup dry white wine

Lemon wedges, for serving

These irresistible snacks are inspired by my time in Italy, where you can find raiche alla giudia (Roman-style Jewish artichokes) on the menus of restaurants in the Jewish quarter in the springtime. Perfectly salty, crispy artichokes in season, served with a super garlicky herb-spiked sauce are otherworldly. This is not the simplest recipe, I'll admit. The artichokes have to be trimmed, which can be a tedious task, and then they are deep-fried—twice. But I'm willing to go through the hassle, because beautifully golden artichokes are one of life's great pleasures.

Preheat the oven to 400°F

Make the Sauce: Cut about ¼ inch off the top of the head of garlic, exposing the cloves but leaving the root intact. Set cut side up on a small square of foil, drizzle with olive oil, season with salt and pepper, and then wrap in foil and roast until the cloves are softened, about 30 to 40 minutes. Let cool for a few minutes, and then unwrap, squeeze the cloves out into a small bowl, and mash to a paste.

Melt the butter in a medium saucepan over medium heat. When the butter is melted, whisk in the flour and cook until the mixture is bubbling, slightly golden, and fragrant. Add the milk, lemon zest, tarragon, and a pinch of salt, and cook, whisking constantly, until thickened, about 6 to 8 minutes. Stir in the Parmesan and a generous pinch of pepper. Set aside.

Prepare the Artichokes: In a large bowl, stir the lemon juice into 2 quarts of water. Using a paring knife, clean the artichokes by cutting away the tough green outer leaves, exposing the delicate internal leaves. Carefully trim the purple part of each leaf, and then trim the ends of the stem. The artichoke will look like an unopened rosebud. Add the artichokes to the bowl of lemon water and cover with a towel to keep them submerged. Let stand for 10 minutes. Remove the artichokes from the water and dry completely with paper towel. Carefully tap them against one another so the leaves begin to open.

Line a baking sheet with paper towel. Heat the grapeseed oil in a large Dutch oven or high-sided, heavy-bottomed pot over medium heat until the oil reaches 300°F on a deep-frying thermometer. Add the artichokes and fry until just knife tender, about 10 minutes. Remove with tongs and set stem side up on the prepared baking sheet; let cool for 15 minutes. Use a fork to open the leaves from the inside to get the shape of a fully bloomed rose. Season with salt and a good bit of pepper.

Increase the oil temperature to 350°F. Sprinkle the artichokes with white wine, and fry a second time until crispy and golden, about 1½ to 2 minutes. Return to the prepared baking sheet to drain, and sprinkle with salt. Serve right away, with lemon wedges and garlic tarragon sauce alongside.

Carrot and Coriander Fritters with Turmeric Yogurt

For the fritters

1½ teaspoons coriander seeds

2 teaspoons fennel seeds

1½ teaspoons cumin seeds

2 cups shredded carrots
(about 3 medium carrots, peeled)

½ white onion, thinly sliced

1 tablespoon grated fresh ginger

3 tablespoons chopped fresh
cilantro

2 large eggs, lightly whisked

1 cup all-purpose flour

½ teaspoon baking powder

Sea salt

Grapeseed oil or other neutral oil,
for frying

For the yogurt sauce

1 cup full-fat Greek yogurt

2 tablespoons honey

Zest of 1 lime

1 tablespoon freshly squeezed
lime juice

1½ teaspoons ground turmeric

Sea salt

For serving

2 tablespoons chopped
fresh cilantro

2 limes, cut into wedges

The humble carrot simply doesn't get enough love. This recipe is a fantastic way to transform a workaday vegetable that I almost always have on hand into the star of the show. The combination of shredded carrots, toasted spices, and fresh ginger and cilantro is a flavor explosion. I especially like them with a dollop of golden turmeric-spiked yogurt, but you could swap in some prepared harissa paste for the turmeric for a spicier condiment.

Preheat the oven to 200°F. Line a baking sheet with paper towel and place in the oven.

Make the Fritters: Heat a small skillet over medium heat and drop in the coriander, fennel, and cumin seeds. Toast, shaking the skillet slightly, until the spices are fragrant and just slightly colored, about 4 to 5 minutes.

In a medium bowl, combine the carrots, onion, ginger, cilantro, and the toasted spices. Add the eggs and stir to mix. In a separate bowl, combine the flour and baking powder, season well with salt, and stir to mix. Add the flour mixture to the carrot mixture and stir to combine.

In a large nonstick skillet over medium heat, pour the grapeseed oil to a depth of a ¼ inch. When the oil is hot, drop 2-tablespoon portions of the carrot mixture into the skillet, flattening them slightly with the back of a spoon. Fry, flipping halfway through, until crispy, golden, and cooked through, about 3 to 4 minutes. Using a slotted spoon, transfer the fritters to the prepared baking sheet in the oven to keep warm. Continue cooking in batches until all the batter has been used.

Make the Yogurt Sauce: In a small bowl, stir together the yogurt, honey, lime zest, lime juice, and turmeric. Season to taste with salt.

Transfer the carrot fritters to a platter and sprinkle with salt and 2 tablespoons of cilantro. Serve with the yogurt and lime wedges alongside.

Salt

Salt. The most important ingredient in any dish. You've no doubt noticed something while reading through this book—there are few specific salt measurements listed. The perfect amount of seasoning, as I see it, is specific to your taste buds. And everyone is wonderfully unique! Sea salt is my personal preference, unless I'm raining a lovely finishing salt (like fleur de sel or flaky salt) on a juicy, perfectly cooked steak or piece of fish. What's perfect for me may be too salty or not salty enough for you and yours. Learning the art of proper seasoning means tasting often and seasoning throughout the cooking process, rather than simply dropping a pinch or two into the pot just before plating up. Tasting at every step along the way to ensure that your seasoning is on point is a vital step in guaranteeing best results.

Kosher salt, used several times throughout this book (and the beloved choice of many), is a beautiful seasoning agent. Not all kosher salt, however, is created equal. The saltiness of each brand can vary greatly, so choosing a specific brand you love and sticking to it is key. In my kitchen, I only use Diamond Crystal Kosher Salt, as it's slightly crumbly, less salty, and dissolves quickly into food, making it the perfect salt for seasoning throughout the cooking process, without overseasoning your dish.

Seasonal Salads and Succulent Sidekicks

My idea of a picture-perfect sunny Saturday morning is waking up early (well, not too early), listening to Chet Baker croon while sipping a creamy cappuccino, and then heading to the farmer's market. Wandering from stall to stall, saying hello to the farmers I know, picking out seasonal bags of tender lettuces, bunches of beets with their lush greens still intact, a masterfully baked baguette, honey from local bees, locally raised meat, and a wheel of my favorite goat's milk cheese. And, practically speaking, it's the best place to load up on the freshest fruits and vegetables in season. They haven't been trucked from 1000 miles away, you'll find things you aren't likely to get at a supermarket, and often the prices are better too. And, ultimately, local in-season food will always taste better.

There can be, of course, too much of a good thing, and often I can't resist the temptations of the market, coming back home with overstuffed bags. And while we might think of vegetables primarily in the warmer months, this chapter has vegetable recipes for every season: from a Confit Tomato, Grilled Peach, and Burrata Salad (page 44) that's perfect for the dog days of summer to Grilled Cabbage Wedges with Spicy Buttermilk-Blue Cheese Dressing (page 55) that's a fine way to round out a winter feast. There's a gratin that uses up a glut of zucchini (page 59), a few ways to dress up the humble but mighty potatoes, including Tartiflette (page 56), which gives the humble tuber the bacon-and-cheese VIP treatment, and boldly flavored sides, like Spicy Gochujang Green Beans (page 60), all of which will make eating your vegetables pure pleasure.

Roasted Squash and Heirloom Tomato Panzanella

½ pound ciabatta loaf, torn into 1-inch pieces

5 tablespoons extra-virgin olive oil, divided

2 tablespoons chopped fresh rosemary

Sea salt and freshly ground black pepper

4 cups (about 2½ pounds) butternut squash, cut into 1-inch cubes

1 pound baby golden beets, peeled and quartered

For the vinaigrette

1 garlic clove, minced

1 shallot, very finely chopped

2 tablespoons apple cider vinegar

1 tablespoon freshly squeezed lemon juice

1 tablespoon pure maple syrup

2 teaspoons whole-grain mustard

⅓ cup extra-virgin olive oil

Sea salt and freshly ground black pepper

For assembly

1 pound mixed heirloom tomatoes, cored and quartered

½ cup pumpkin seeds, toasted

½ cup crumbled fresh goat cheese (chèvre)

¼ cup minced fresh basil

Fresh flat-leaf parsley, for garnish (optional)

I was introduced to panzanella when I first visited the Tuscan countryside. A rustic, humble tomato-based salad created to give new life to day-old bread. My version is a shoulder season salad, perfect for those late summer days when the farmer's markets are loaded with jewel-toned heirloom tomatoes but the first hard squash begin appearing alongside, signifying that fall isn't too far away. The marriage of juicy heirloom tomatoes and sweet roasted squash is magical. Though it's not traditional, I like to add goat cheese to my panzanella, along with toasted pumpkin seeds for a little crunch. Perfect paired with a glass of Pinot and enjoyed al fresco under the autumn sun.

Preheat the oven (or grill if cooking outside, which I highly recommend) to 350°F. Line 2 large baking sheets with parchment paper.

On one of the prepared baking sheets, combine the bread, 3 tablespoons of the olive oil, and the rosemary, season with salt and pepper, and toss to coat. On the second prepared baking sheet, combine the squash and beets, drizzle with the remaining 2 tablespoons of the olive oil, and season with salt and pepper. Toss to coat. Transfer both baking sheets to the oven.

Bake the croutons for 20 to 25 minutes, tossing halfway through, until crispy and golden brown. Cook the vegetables for 35 to 40 minutes, tossing halfway through, until the squash is tender and golden brown and the beets are cooked through and fork-tender. Let the vegetables cool until just warm.

Make the Vinaigrette: In a medium bowl, whisk together the garlic, shallot, vinegar, lemon juice, syrup, and mustard. In a slow and steady stream, and while constantly whisking, add the olive oil until the vinaigrette is thickened and emulsified. Season to taste with salt and pepper.

In a large bowl, combine the roasted vegetables, tomatoes, pumpkin seeds, goat cheese, basil, and croutons. Drizzle the vinaigrette and toss to mix well. Plate the panzanella, garnish with parsley (if using), and serve warm.

Confit Tomato, Grilled Peach, and Burrata Salad

2 pounds mixed cherry tomatoes

6 garlic cloves, peeled and gently crushed

4 sprigs fresh thyme

4 sprigs fresh rosemary

Sea salt and freshly ground black pepper

Extra-virgin olive oil

2 large ripe peaches (about ½ pound), halved and pitted

2 tablespoons minced fresh basil, plus more whole leaves for garnish

2 tablespoons Champagne vinegar

1 tablespoon freshly squeezed lemon juice

2 balls (each 8 ounces) burrata

Tomatoes and burrata is a classic combination. And for good reason: it's perfection in a bite. To make this salad extra special, I also add wedges of grilled peaches and cook the tomatoes in a low-heat oven with a lot of olive oil until they're soft and all their sweetness has been concentrated (this trick enhances even humdrum tomatoes—a perfect hack). Don't throw out the oil from the cooked tomatoes—it's a flavor enhancer par excellence, wonderful drizzled on soup, pasta, or risotto, or used to make a vinaigrette.

Preheat the oven to 275°F.

Combine the tomatoes, garlic, thyme, and rosemary in a high-sided baking dish. Season with salt and pepper, and pour in enough olive oil to cover the small tomatoes and go halfway up the larger tomatoes. Roast until the tomatoes are wilted but not blistered, about 1½ to 2 hours. Let cool to room temperature, remove the garlic (reserve for the vinaigrette), and remove and discard the herbs. Using a slotted spoon, transfer the tomatoes to a large serving platter. Reserve 3 tablespoons of the oil, and transfer the rest to a lidded jar, chill in the fridge, and save for another use. I love drizzling this oil on soups, over pasta, or whisked into a vinaigrette. Oil will keep in an airtight container for about 1 week, though it definitely won't last that long.

Preheat a grill for direct, medium-heat grilling (see Notes on Grilling, page 187). Place the peach halves directly on the grill grate and grill, turning occasionally, until tender and lightly charred in spots, about 4 to 5 minutes. Remove from the grill and, when cool enough to handle, cut into wedges.

In a large bowl, use a fork to mash the reserved garlic into a paste. Whisk in the basil, vinegar, lemon juice, and the 3 tablespoons of reserved oil. Season to taste with a pinch of salt.

Arrange the grilled peaches and burrata over the tomatoes, drizzle the vinaigrette, and garnish with fresh basil. Season with additional salt and pepper to taste, and serve.

Chicory Caesar with Anchovy Fritters

For the fritters

½ cup all-purpose flour

½ cup cornmeal

1 teaspoon baking soda

1 teaspoon baking powder

⅓ cup grated Parmesan cheese

Zest of 1 lemon

Sea salt and freshly ground black pepper

¼ cup whole milk

¼ cup buttermilk

1 large egg

10 oil-packed anchovy fillets, chopped

Grapeseed oil or other neutral oil, for frying

For the salad

8 strips bacon (about 8 ounces)

2 oil-packed anchovy fillets

1 large egg yolk

1 small shallot, coarsely chopped

2 garlic cloves, chopped

1 tablespoon Dijon mustard

1 tablespoon sherry vinegar

1 tablespoon freshly squeezed lemon juice

Sea salt and freshly ground black pepper

1 cup extra-virgin olive oil

⅓ cup finely grated Parmesan cheese, plus lots more for garnish

4 heads endive, chopped

2 heads escarole, tough outer leaves removed, torn

The classics. Those dishes that are timeless, chock-full of nostalgia, and, of course, eternally delicious. It's hard to improve on a classic Caesar salad, the stalwart of room service menus and steakhouses. But this version—where romaine lettuce is swapped for equally crisp but more flavorful endive and escarole, and anchovies are introduced in the form of fluffy, crunchy fritters—is a worthy rendition. You can wash the greens, prepare the dressing, and mix the fritter batter in advance, but don't fry the fritters until just before you plan to serve the salad, or they'll become soggy. And did I mention this Caesar has a bacon garnish? As we all know, bacon makes everything better.

Preheat the oven to 350°F.

Make the Fritters: In a medium bowl, whisk together the flour, cornmeal, baking soda, baking powder, Parmesan, lemon zest, and a pinch each of salt and pepper. In a second bowl, combine the milk, buttermilk, egg, and chopped anchovies, and mix well. Stir the wet ingredients into the dry until combined. Cover and set aside.

Make the Salad: Line a plate with paper towels and set nearby. Lay the bacon in a single layer on a parchment-lined baking sheet. Bake, turning halfway through, for 25 to 30 minutes, until crispy and golden brown. With tongs, transfer the cooked bacon to the prepared plate to drain. Crumble into small bits and set aside.

In a blender, combine the anchovies, egg yolk, shallot, garlic, mustard, vinegar, lemon juice, and a pinch of salt and pepper. Pulse until smooth. With the machine running on low speed, drizzle in the oil in a slow and steady stream until completely incorporated. Transfer to a bowl and stir in the Parmesan.

Fry the Fritters: In a large Dutch oven or high-sided, heavy-bottomed pot, pour the grapeseed oil to a depth of 3 inches. Heat over medium heat until the oil reaches 350°F on a deep-frying thermometer. Line a plate with paper towels and set nearby. Working in batches, drop 1-tablespoon portions of batter into the oil and fry, turning halfway through, for 1 to 2 minutes, until crispy and golden brown. With a spider or slotted spoon, transfer to the prepared plate. Repeat with the remaining batter until all the fritters have been fried, letting the oil return to 350°F between each batch.

Assemble the Salad: In a large salad bowl, combine the endive and escarole. Add half the dressing and toss well to coat; add additional dressing to taste. Any leftover dressing can be stored in an airtight container in the refrigerator for up to 3 days.

Transfer the salad to a large serving platter (or individual plates), and top with bacon bits and loads of Parmesan cheese. Go heavy with the Parmesan, friends. Top with the anchovy fritters and a few cracks of black pepper.

Fattoush with Grilled Halloumi and Eggplant

For the dressing

¼ cup extra-virgin olive oil

3 tablespoons freshly squeezed lemon juice

1 garlic clove, minced

1 teaspoon sumac

Pinch of sugar

Sea salt and freshly ground black pepper

For the fattoush

⅓ cup plus 1 tablespoon extra-virgin olive oil, divided

3 tablespoons za'atar

4 garlic cloves, minced

Sea salt

2 medium eggplants, cut into ½-inch-thick rounds

1 medium red onion, peeled and sliced into thin rounds

2 large pita breads, cut into small triangles

8 ounces halloumi cheese, cut into 8 thick slices

1 green pepper, diced

1 English cucumber, diced

2 cups cherry tomatoes, halved

2 cups chopped green leaf or romaine lettuce

½ cup fresh parsley, chopped

¼ cup fresh dill, chopped, plus more for garnish

¼ cup fresh mint, chopped, plus more for garnish

½ cup pitted kalamata olives

Lemon wedges, for serving

I absolutely love the marriage of toasty grilled bread and crisp, fresh vegetables in salads. My take on this vibrant Levantine salad combines crispy pieces of pita with grilled and fresh vegetables, all tossed in a lemony dressing that gets some tanginess from the addition of sumac, a brick-red spice with a tart, lemony flavor. The fresh herbs—a mixture of parsley, dill, and mint—are vital to this salad, and I also add za'atar, a spice blend of wild thyme and sesame that can be purchased at well-stocked grocery stores. Halloumi, for the uninitiated, is a wonderful salty cow's milk cheese that can be grilled without melting (miraculous!).

Make the Dressing: In a medium bowl, whisk together the olive oil, lemon juice, garlic, sumac, and a pinch of sugar. Season to taste with salt and pepper. Easy-peasy. Set aside.

Preheat a grill for direct, medium-high heat grilling (see Notes on Grilling, page 187).

Make the Fattoush: In a small bowl, mix together ⅓ cup of the olive oil, the za'atar, garlic, and a pinch of salt until smooth. Brush the oil mixture on both sides of the eggplant, onion, and pita, and then grill until golden and slightly charred on both sides, about 5 to 7 minutes for the vegetables and 2 to 3 minutes for the pita. Keep a close watch as the pita will be done several minutes before the vegetables; when the pita is done, transfer it to a rimmed baking sheet and break into bite-size pieces. Transfer the vegetables to the baking sheet when they are ready.

Brush the halloumi with the remaining 1 tablespoon of olive oil. Grill, turning halfway through, until golden all over, with beautiful char marks on both sides. Transfer to the rimmed baking sheet with the vegetables and pita.

On a large serving platter, arrange the green pepper, cucumber, tomatoes, lettuce, parsley, dill, mint, and olives. Add the grilled eggplant, onion, pita, and halloumi. Add the dressing and mix well, making sure that lemony goodness coats everything completely. Garnish with fresh dill and mint leaves, and serve with lemon wedges.

Nicoise Salad with Blackened Trout

1 pound baby new potatoes, rinsed but not peeled

⅓ cup plus 1 tablespoon extra-virgin olive oil, divided

½ pound green beans, trimmed

4 large eggs

1 garlic clove, minced

1 medium shallot, minced

1 tablespoon Dijon mustard

2 tablespoons freshly squeezed lemon juice

Sea salt and freshly ground black pepper

Zest of 1 lemon

1 teaspoon smoked paprika

½ teaspoon cayenne pepper

1 teaspoon dried oregano

1 teaspoon packed brown sugar

1 pound rainbow trout fillet

2 tablespoons grapeseed oil or other neutral oil

2 tablespoons butter

2 cups pea shoots (or your favorite greens)

1 cup halved cherry tomatoes

½ cup shelled fresh peas

½ cup pitted kalamata olives

½ cup chopped fresh basil

1 lemon, cut into wedges, for serving

Inspired by Provençal tuna Niçoise and hearty enough to be a light dinner, this salad is loaded with vegetables, brightened with basil and a zippy vinaigrette, and enriched by the addition of eggs and pan-fried trout—a more sustainable (and affordable) alternative to tuna. Serve it with some crusty bread and a bottle of chilled rosé.

Place the potatoes in a large saucepan and add cold water to cover by a few inches. Generously salt the water. Boil over high heat until the potatoes are tender, about 12 to 15 minutes (to check for doneness, pierce a potato with the tip of a sharp knife; it should slide in easily). Drain, transfer to a bowl, and toss with 1 tablespoon of the olive oil. Set aside.

Bring a medium saucepan of salted water to a boil over high heat. Add the green beans and cook until crisp-tender, about 4 minutes. Remove with a spider or tongs (do not drain the water), run under cold water until cool, and set aside.

Carefully add the eggs to the boiling water from the green beans, and set a timer for 7 minutes. (Preference is key here, but for my boiled eggs, I love a cooked white and a gloriously gooey yolk. If you enjoy your boiled eggs a little more cooked through, add 30 to 45 seconds to the cooking time.) Prepare an ice water bath. When the timer goes off, remove your eggs from the water with a spider or slotted spoon, and transfer to the prepared ice bath. Let stand until cool enough to handle, and then peel.

Whisk together the garlic, shallot, and mustard in a medium bowl set on a damp towel (this will help prevent it from moving while you whisk). While constantly whisking, slowly stream in the remaining ⅓ cup olive oil, whisking until thick and emulsified. Whisk in the lemon juice and season to taste with salt and pepper. Set the vinaigrette aside.

In a small bowl, stir together the lemon zest, paprika, cayenne, oregano, brown sugar, and a generous pinch of salt and pepper. Rub the flesh side of the trout all over with the spice mixture, coating it completely. Heat the grapeseed oil in a large, high-sided skillet over medium heat until the oil is shimmering. Carefully add the trout flesh side down and cook for 2 to 3 minutes, until golden and starting to blacken. Carefully flip, and then add the butter. Continue to cook, basting the fish with the melted butter, until the trout is cooked through and easily flakes with a fork, about 2 to 3 more minutes. Transfer to a cutting board.

On a large serving platter, spread a bed of pea shoots. Top with the potatoes, green beans, cherry tomatoes, peas, and olives, arranging them artfully around the perimeter of the serving dish. Place the trout in the center, and then halve the eggs and set them on top. Garnish with the basil, and drizzle with the vinaigrette. Season with salt and pepper, and serve with lemon wedges.

Maritime Potluck Potato Salad

2½ pounds Yukon Gold potatoes, peeled

Sea salt

3 tablespoons Champagne vinegar

1 teaspoon Dijon mustard

2 garlic cloves, minced

1 large egg yolk, at room temperature

¾ cup extra-virgin olive oil

Freshly ground black pepper

½ cup thinly sliced green onions

½ cup finely chopped celery

½ medium red onion, finely chopped

¾ pound cooked lobster meat, cut into 1-inch pieces

¾ pound cooked picked crab meat, cut into 1-inch pieces

Zest and juice of 1 lemon

2 tablespoons chopped fresh tarragon

2 tablespoons chopped fresh chives

A proper potato salad is one of life's great pleasures. Served in the Maritimes alongside crispy fried seafood or a big bucket of Dixie Lee fried chicken, and found at literally every potluck from Lamèque to Yarmouth, it's pure comfort food. Though potato salad is forever the sidekick, I love elevating simple dishes to hero status, and this recipe certainly delivers. Admittedly, this is a luxurious potato salad, one that speaks to the part of the world where I'm from, where snow crab and lobster are ubiquitous (and less expensive than they might be in other parts of the world). But if you're looking for a fancy twist on workaday potato salad, give it a shot. Because it's so rich, you might serve this with some dressed greens and boiled corn alongside for a complete summertime, patio-friendly supper.

Place the potatoes in a large pot and add cold water to cover them by a few inches. Generously salt the water, and bring to a boil over high heat. Lower the heat to medium, and let the spuds simmer away until just fork-tender, about 15 to 20 minutes. Cooking time will entirely depend on the size of your potatoes. Keep an eye out at the 15-minute mark so you don't overcook them. Drain the potatoes, quarter them, and transfer to a large bowl.

While the potatoes are cooking, make the dressing. In a large bowl set on a damp towel (this will prevent the bowl from moving as you whisk), whisk together the vinegar, mustard, garlic, and egg yolk until frothy. Add the oil in a slow, steady stream, whisking constantly, until thick and emulsified. Season to taste with salt and pepper.

Add about half of the dressing to the hot potatoes so the spuds will absorb all that flavor. To the bowl with the potatoes, add the green onions, celery, and red onion. Stir to combine. Add the lobster, crab, lemon zest and juice, tarragon, chives, and the remaining dressing, and give everything a gentle mix. Taste and adjust the seasoning as necessary. Cover and chill in the fridge for about an hour before serving. Any leftovers can be stored in an airtight container in the refrigerator for up to 2 days (though it certainly won't last that long).

Grilled Cabbage Wedges with Spicy Buttermilk-Blue Cheese Dressing

For the salad

1 large savoy cabbage, rough outer leaves removed and cut into wedges

3 tablespoons extra-virgin olive oil

Sea salt and freshly ground black pepper

2 cups walnut halves

⅓ cup pure maple syrup

1 teaspoon smoked paprika

For the dressing

2 jalapeño peppers

1 cup buttermilk

¼ cup sour cream

¼ cup mayonnaise, homemade (page 118) or store-bought

2 tablespoons finely chopped fresh dill, plus more for garnish

2 tablespoons finely chopped fresh chives, plus more for garnish

2 tablespoons finely chopped fresh flat-leaf parsley

2 teaspoons onion powder

½ cup crumbled blue cheese, divided

Sea salt and freshly ground black pepper

In wintertime, salad options become more limited, especially on the snowy east coast of Canada—all flavorless tomatoes and sad lettuce. But cabbage shines this time of year—it's inexpensive, reliably good, and wonderful in this salad, where wedges are grilled until sweet and lightly charred. Look for savoy cabbage, which is a green variety with ruffled leaves that's slightly sweeter than your standard green cabbage. If you can't find it, though, you can certainly substitute green cabbage. For the dressing, use a crumbly, rather than creamy, blue cheese. Cabbage and blue cheese = a match made in heaven.

Make the Salad: Brush the cabbage wedges all over with the olive oil, coating well, and season all over with salt and pepper. Let sit for 1 hour.

Heat a medium skillet over medium heat. Add the walnuts, syrup, paprika, and a pinch of salt. Cook, stirring often, until the syrup has thickened, coating the walnuts, and the walnuts are toasted, about 3 to 4 minutes. Transfer to a plate, spread in a single layer, and let cool.

Preheat a grill for direct, medium-high heat grilling (see Notes on Grilling, page 187).

Place the jalapeños directly on the grill grates and cook until blistered and charred all over. With tongs, transfer to a plate and let cool. Wearing plastic gloves, stem, seed and finely chop the peppers.

Place the cabbage wedges directly on the grill grates and cook, turning halfway through, until crispy and golden on the outside and softened on the inside, about 12 to 15 minutes.

Make the Dressing: While the cabbage is cooking, whisk together the buttermilk, sour cream, mayonnaise, dill, chives, parsley, onion powder, ¼ cup of the blue cheese, and the chopped jalapeños. Season to taste with salt and pepper.

Transfer the cabbage wedges to a serving platter, and spoon the dressing over. Top with the caramelized walnuts and the remaining ¼ cup of the blue cheese. Garnish with dill and chives and serve.

Tartiflette

2½ pounds unpeeled baby
new potatoes

1 tablespoon extra-virgin olive oil

8 ounces bacon, roughly chopped

2 large white onions, thinly sliced

1 tablespoon fresh thyme, chopped

Sea salt

2 garlic cloves, minced

¾ cup dry white wine

1 tablespoon unsalted butter

⅓ cup heavy (35%) cream

Freshly ground black pepper

1 pound Reblochon cheese, sliced
into thin strips (or substitute with
fontina, Gruyère, or even Brie)

If you're looking for rib-sticking food and cold-weather comfort, you
need look no further than the Alps, where the locals have perfected
the art of meals showcasing potatoes, cured meat, and cheese.
Tartiflette, a sort of potato casserole that originated in the Savoy
region of France, is one of the finest examples and a wonderful
thing to make when it's snowing sideways. Tartiflette is traditionally
made with Reblochon, a washed-rind cow's milk cheese with an
assertive flavor and distinct creaminess. If you can find it, by all
means use it for this recipe. If not, you can substitute another
mountain cheese that melts well, such as fontina or Gruyère. And
if you want a vegetarian version, simply omit the bacon; it won't
be traditional, but it'll still taste great. Because this is rich, I like to
serve it with a big green salad with a zippy, acidic vinaigrette.

Preheat the oven to 400°F.

Place the potatoes in a large saucepan and add water to cover
by a few inches. Generously salt the water and bring to a boil over
medium-high heat. Cook until the potatoes are just fork-tender, about
10 to 15 minutes. Drain and let cool.

Heat the olive oil in a large skillet over medium heat until the oil is
shimmering. Carefully add the bacon and cook until it is just starting
to become golden, about 5 to 6 minutes. Remove the bacon with a
slotted spoon and set aside. Add the onions and thyme to the skillet.
Season with a pinch of salt and cook, stirring, until the onions are
softened and translucent, about 6 to 8 minutes. Add the garlic and
cook for 30 seconds. Pour in the white wine and cook for an additional
2 minutes. Add the butter to the skillet and let it melt into the oniony
wine mixture. Remove from the heat.

Spread the potatoes in a 14 x 10-inch (4-quart) baking or casserole dish.
Spoon in the onion mixture, bacon, and cream, and season with salt
and pepper. Stir to mix, making sure that your potatoes are completely
coated in oniony, bacony, creamy deliciousness. Top with the Reblochon
cheese, and bake until the cheese is melted, golden, bubbly, and
caramelized at the edges, 30 to 35 minutes.

Zucchini, Blue Cheese, and Leek Gratin

5 tablespoons extra-virgin olive oil, divided

½ cup panko breadcrumbs

Zest of 1 lemon, divided

2 tablespoons chopped fresh tarragon

Sea salt

2 leeks, white and light green parts only, sliced

1 teaspoon red pepper flakes

4 garlic cloves, minced

3 medium zucchini, grated

½ cup crumbled blue cheese

¾ cup heavy (35%) cream

Freshly ground black pepper

1 medium zucchini, thinly sliced

1 cup grated whole-milk mozzarella

¼ cup fresh basil, chopped

Zucchini is kind of like the joke vegetable of summer. A delicious joke, but still. There's always too much of it growing in the garden— you might have a friend or neighbor who is always trying to gift you some before it becomes the size of baseball bats. And sure, yes, zucchini bread is good, but how much of that can you bake? This lush gratin is a wonderful way to elevate that zucchini you've just been gifted. I love the contrast of the sweet leeks and salty assertive blue cheese against the mellow squash. But if you're not a blue cheese lover, no worries. Substitute another cheese instead—an aged cheddar would also be great.

Preheat the oven to 350°F and lightly oil a 9-inch square baking dish.

In a small bowl, combine 2 tablespoons of the olive oil, the breadcrumbs, half the lemon zest, tarragon, and a small pinch of salt, and mix until every crumb is coated in oil.

Heat 2 tablespoons of the olive oil in a medium skillet over medium heat until the oil is shimmering. Carefully add the leeks and red pepper flakes, season with a pinch of salt, and cook, stirring occasionally, until softened, about 10 to 12 minutes. Add the garlic and cook for an additional 2 minutes, until fragrant, then remove from the heat.

Place the grated zucchini in a kitchen towel and, working over the sink in batches, squeeze hard to remove any excess liquid. Really get in there, friends, and squeeze with all your might. We want all that liquid gone.

In a medium bowl, mix together the grated zucchini, leek mixture, blue cheese, remaining lemon zest, and heavy cream. Season with salt and pepper, and mix well. Spoon the mixture into the prepared baking dish. Toss the sliced zucchini with the remaining 1 tablespoon of olive oil, and season with a pinch of salt. Arrange the slices on top of the baking dish in an even layer, covering the surface completely. Top with the mozzarella, followed by the breadcrumb mixture, and a crack or two of pepper. Bake until golden and bubbling, about 25 to 30 minutes, then top with fresh basil.

Should you be blessed with any leftovers, store them in an airtight container in the refrigerator for up to 3 days. To reheat, simply bake in a preheated oven at 350°F until the cheese is melted and bubbly.

Spicy Gochujang Green Beans

2 tablespoons gochujang

1 tablespoon rice vinegar

1 tablespoon pure maple syrup

¼ cup plus 2 tablespoons vegetable stock, divided

1 garlic clove, minced

1 pound green beans, trimmed

1 tablespoon grapeseed oil or other neutral oil

Sea salt

¼ cup roasted salted peanuts, chopped

2 teaspoons toasted sesame seeds

2 green onions, finely sliced

¼ cup minced fresh cilantro

I adore green beans! When I first started a backyard garden, only two things had a successful season—green beans and my farming education (I learned . . . a lot). Freshly picked, they are a thing of real beauty (and the perfect while-you-weed-the-garden snack). This quick side is one of my favorite ways to prepare them. The gochujang, a spicy Korean red pepper paste, kisses the beans with some gentle heat, balanced by the sweetness of maple syrup and some acidity from the rice vinegar. Serve these beans with the Sriracha Maple Salmon (page 169), the Hoisin Pork Meatballs (page 231), or the Miso Marinated Grilled Chicken (page 215).

In a small bowl, whisk together the gochujang, vinegar, syrup, 2 tablespoons of the stock, and the garlic.

In a large skillet (or wok) over high heat, bring the remaining ¼ cup of the stock to a boil. Add the beans, cover, and cook for 4 minutes. Remove the lid and stir the beans, allowing any remaining stock to cook off until the skillet is dry.

Pour in the oil, season with a pinch of salt, and continue cooking until the beans are blistered and slightly charred on both sides, about 3 to 4 minutes. Pour in the gochujang sauce, give everything a good stir, and continue cooking for 1 minute, until crisp-tender and charred in spots. Season to taste with additional salt, transfer to a serving platter, and top with the peanuts, sesame seeds, green onions, and cilantro.

Garlicky Broccoli Rabe with Toasted Breadcrumbs

4 slices day-old sourdough bread, crusts removed and roughly chopped

5 tablespoons extra-virgin olive oil, divided

1 tablespoon unsalted butter

2 garlic cloves, minced

2 teaspoons chopped fresh thyme

1 tablespoon minced fresh flat-leaf parsley, plus more for garnish

⅓ cup finely grated pecorino Romano cheese

Sea salt and freshly ground black pepper

2 pounds broccoli rabe, trimmed and chopped

6 garlic cloves, thinly sliced

6 anchovy fillets, chopped

¼ teaspoon crushed red pepper flakes

2 teaspoons freshly squeezed lemon juice

I love the bitter flavor of broccoli rabe, also known as rapini. To tenderize and slightly neutralize its bitterness, it's first blanched and then sautéed in garlicky olive oil. For a finishing touch, the greens are dusted with cheesy, crunchy breadcrumbs. Even if you think you don't like anchovies, don't omit them—they melt into the oil, giving the breadcrumbs a deeply savory and addictive flavor. If you don't have anchovies, you can substitute a splash of fish sauce.

In a food processor, pulse the bread until breadcrumbs form. Heat 2 tablespoons of the olive oil and the butter in a skillet over medium heat. When the butter has melted, add the minced garlic and thyme and cook for 30 seconds, keeping a close watch so the garlic doesn't burn. Add the breadcrumbs and cook, stirring often, until golden and toasted, about 5 minutes. Remove from the heat and stir in the parsley and pecorino. Season to taste with salt and pepper and set aside.

Bring a large pot of salted water to a boil. Add the broccoli rabe and cook for 2 minutes. Drain and set aside. When it's cool enough to handle, squeeze the broccoli rabe to remove excess water.

Heat the remaining 3 tablespoons of the olive oil in a skillet over medium heat until the oil is shimmering. Carefully add the sliced garlic, anchovies, and red pepper flakes. Cook, stirring, for 1 minute, until the garlic is just beginning to turn golden. Add the broccoli rabe, toss to coat in the garlicky oil, and cook for 3 to 5 minutes longer, until tender. Add the lemon juice and season to taste with salt and pepper.

Transfer to a serving dish, top with the breadcrumbs, and garnish with the parsley.

Miso Butter Mushrooms with Garlic Bok Choy

For the bok choy

1 tablespoon grapeseed oil or other neutral oil

1 tablespoon toasted sesame oil

10 green onions, trimmed and cut crosswise into 3-inch pieces

5 garlic cloves, minced

1 pound bok choy, end trimmed and leaves separated

2 tablespoons soy sauce

For the mushrooms

2 tablespoons grapeseed oil or other neutral oil

2 tablespoons minced fresh ginger

4 garlic cloves, peeled and very thinly sliced

2 bird's eye or Thai chilies, stemmed, seeded, and thinly sliced

2 tablespoons minced fresh cilantro stems

1 pound mixed mushrooms (I like shiitake, portobello, and oyster mushrooms), stems trimmed, larger mushrooms sliced and smaller mushrooms left whole

½ cup vegetable or porcini stock, homemade (page 109) or store-bought

2 tablespoons unsalted butter

2 tablespoons soy sauce

¼ cup red miso

¼ cup Shaoxing rice wine or dry sherry

2 teaspoons pure maple syrup

For serving

2 tablespoons toasted sesame seeds

2 tablespoons chopped fresh cilantro

Steamed jasmine rice

Miso is one of those amazing flavor-enhancing ingredients that once you start using, you kind of want to add to . . . everything. Miso ice cream, anyone? Made from salted, fermented soybeans, it adds nutty sweetness and further boosts the natural umami-rich flavor of the mushrooms in this dish. I pile the mushrooms on top of simple sautéed bok choy and serve it as a side dish, but with some steamed rice alongside (and maybe some chili crunch) this dish becomes a satisfying veggie-forward main course.

Prepare the Bok Choy: Heat the grapeseed and sesame oils in a wok or large skillet over medium-high heat until the oils are shimmering. Carefully add the green onions and garlic and cook, stirring, for 30 seconds. Add the bok choy and soy sauce, and cook for 2 to 4 minutes, until the bok choy leaves are wilted but the stems retain some crunch. Transfer the bok choy to a plate and set aside.

Prepare the Mushrooms: Heat the grapeseed oil in the same wok or large skillet over medium-high heat until the oil is shimmering. Carefully add the ginger, garlic, chilies, and cilantro stems, and cook, stirring, for 1 minute. With a slotted spoon, transfer the mixture to a plate; leave the oil in the wok.

Add the mushrooms and cook for about 6 to 8 minutes, stirring, until they're just starting to brown and release their liquid. Add the stock, butter, soy sauce, miso, Shaoxing wine, and syrup, and then return the garlic mixture to the wok and bring to a simmer. Reduce the heat to medium-low so the liquid is simmering gently, and cook for about 25 to 30 minutes, until the sauce is glossy and reduced. Transfer the mushrooms to a serving dish, give the wok a quick clean with paper towels, then add the bok choy back to the wok, and stir to warm for a few minutes, then transfer to a serving dish.

Garnish the mushrooms and bok choy with the toasted sesame seeds and cilantro, and serve with steamed rice.

Roasted Garlic and Goat Cheese Mashed Potatoes

1 head garlic

1 teaspoon extra-virgin olive oil

Sea salt and freshly ground black pepper

3 pounds Yukon Gold potatoes, peeled and roughly chopped

¾ cup heavy (35%) cream

¾ cup crumbled goat cheese (chèvre)

1 tablespoon lemon zest

4 tablespoons unsalted butter, melted, plus more for drizzling

2 tablespoons finely minced fresh chives

Mashed potatoes, bless you. Thank you for existing and making the world a more beautiful place. I believe there is no such thing as too many mashed potato recipes, and these—with a generous amount of roasted garlic, enriched with goat cheese, and brightened with lemon—are a wonderful addition to the side dish canon. They are a perfect addition to a holiday feast: serve them alongside the Turkey Roulade (page 221) or My Favorite Swedish Meatballs (page 228).

Preheat the oven to 350°F.

Using a sharp knife, slice about ¼ inch off the top of the garlic head, exposing the cloves but leaving the root intact. Drizzle the exposed garlic with the olive oil, and season with a pinch of salt and pepper. Tightly wrap the garlic head in aluminum foil, transfer to the oven and roast for 30 to 35 minutes, until the cloves are soft. Let stand until cool enough to handle. Unwrap, squeeze the cloves out into a small bowl, and mash to a paste.

Meanwhile, bring a large pot of salted water to a boil. Add the potatoes and lower the heat to medium-high. Cook for 15 to 20 minutes or until tender. Drain and return to the pot, stirring over low heat until dry. Remove from the heat and stir in the cream, goat cheese, lemon zest, mashed garlic paste, and butter. Mash until smooth. If you like your mashed potatoes extra fluffy, whip that business up with a whisk. Season to taste with salt and pepper. Garnish with the chives, a generous drizzle of melted butter, and an extra crack or two of black pepper.

Roasted Acorn Squash with Sauerkraut, Pomegranate, and Arugula

2 large acorn squash
(about 2 to 3 pounds each)

4 tablespoons unsalted butter, melted

3 tablespoons pure maple syrup

2 teaspoons smoked paprika

¼ teaspoon cayenne pepper

Sea salt and freshly ground black pepper

3 cups baby arugula

2 tablespoons extra-virgin olive oil

2 tablespoons lemon juice

Zest of 1 lemon

2 cups sauerkraut

¼ cup pomegranate arils

This fall-friendly recipe is inspired by my dear friend Chef Conor Spacey. While cooking together at our first Chef's Manifesto Action Hubs in London, he prepared this little gem of a dish for our family-style dinner, and I absolutely loved the combination of sweet roasted squash and salty, tangy sauerkraut. While it's hearty enough to be a stand-alone main course, if you're an omnivore it also pairs perfectly with all sorts of things, from grilled sausages to juicy pork chops to a gorgeous reverse-seared medium-rare steak, like the Bistecca alla Fiorentina (page 253).

Preheat the oven (or grill) to 400°F and line a large baking sheet with parchment paper.

Halve the squash, remove the stem and seeds, and cut into 2-inch wedges. In a small bowl, combine the butter, syrup, paprika, and cayenne, and mix well. Brush the squash wedges all over with the buttery maple mixture, and season all sides with salt and pepper. Arrange on the prepared baking sheet in an even layer.

Roast for 25 to 30 minutes, or until the bottom half of each wedge is golden and starting to caramelize. Flip and continue cooking until all sides are golden brown. Transfer to a platter.

Place your arugula in a medium bowl. Drizzle on the olive oil and lemon juice, add the lemon zest, season with salt and pepper, and toss.

Top the squash with spoonfuls of sauerkraut, the dressed arugula, and the pomegranate arils. Season with salt and pepper and serve warm.

There's Always Room for a Little Pasta

I taly destroyed me, in the best of ways. And from the first moment I touched down in the Bel Paese, that forever-inspiring country shaped how I view food, feed people, and enjoy food around the family table: the emphasis on culinary tradition, the art of taking four or five in-season ingredients and celebrating them at their best, the revelation that feeding someone is an act of love, and the importance of celebrating time spent at the table. And the pasta. The pasta!

How can pasta—something made with only flour, eggs, and a little olive oil—be so damn tasty? It's a marvel. This chapter celebrates that marvel, beginning with a recipe for from-scratch pasta dough (page 75). In addition to fresh pasta, I've also included recipes that call for dry pasta, a versatile, inexpensive staple that I always have in my pantry. I like to stock up on a few different cuts, some long, like spaghetti, and some short, like rigatoni, so I have options when a pasta craving hits (which, honestly, is quite often. Like, often often). When it comes to dry pasta, it's worth spending just a bit more money to get a good-quality brand, preferably one that is bronze-die extruded (this means exactly what it sounds like—the pasta dough is extruded through a bronze die). This gives the pasta a rougher texture, which helps the sauce cling to it.

In this chapter, you'll find my versions of classic pasta dishes, including Rigatoni alla Carbonara (page 91) and Spicy Pasta alla Norma (page 83) as well as some not-yet-classics, like a baked pasta with grilled chicken, spinach, and crème fraîche (page 99) and a tomato-y orzo (the forgotten pasta!) with grilled shrimp and salsa verde (page 84). Because, as we all know, there's no such thing as too much pasta.

Fresh Pasta

14 ounces "00" flour, plus more for dusting

1½ teaspoons kosher salt

4 large eggs

1 tablespoon extra-virgin olive oil

While it might seem intimidating to make fresh pasta, I assure you it's easier than it seems and well worth the effort. Not only is fresh pasta an absolute treat, once you've gotten the hang of it, the possibilities are endless: You can dress the boiled noodles with butter and Parmesan for a simple feast, or use it to make more ambitious pasta preparations, such as Lemony Basil and Ricotta Ravioli (page 76) or a rich layered Sunday Lunch Lasagna (page 101).

Combine the flour and salt on a clean work surface and make a well in the center. Crack the eggs into the well, pour in the olive oil, and lightly beat the eggs and oil together with a fork. Using your fork, start to pull flour from the outside of the well into the center, gradually mixing it together with the eggs. After a few minutes, when the flour is too thick to work with a fork, get your hands in there and start working the dough with your fingertips. When the dough starts to come together, switch to kneading the dough with your hands.

Knead the dough for about 10 minutes, until the dough ball is elastic and smooth. (Hard work? Yes. Counts as going to the gym? Maybe?) Place the dough ball on a floured surface, cover with a damp towel, and let rest at room temperature for 1 hour before rolling. This resting time will help the dough relax and make it much easier to work with.

Divide the dough in half. Lightly flour one of the dough balls and cover with a damp towel. Flatten the other piece into a disk, and use a rolling pin to roll the dough out into a long ¼-inch-thick rectangle that's no wider than your pasta maker. With the pasta machine on the thickest setting, feed the dough through the rollers. Repeat.

Fold the rolled-out piece into thirds and press it between your hands into a disk. Continue passing the dough sheet through the machine, sending it through twice, and then lowering the setting. If the dough sheet becomes too long or hard to manage, cut it in half. Ultimately, the thickness you stop at depends on both your preference and the recipe. I tend to stop on the second last setting on my machine.

At this point the dough can be used in a variety of different ways: cut into noodles of varying thickness, cut into squares and used to make tortellini, or filled and folded to make ravioli (see page 76). Tightly wrap the dough in plastic wrap and store in the refrigerator for up to 2 days.

Lemony Basil and Ricotta Ravioli

1 batch fresh pasta dough (page 75)

20 ounces fresh whole-milk ricotta cheese, drained

¾ cup finely grated Parmesan cheese, divided

Zest of 1 lemon

1 tablespoon plus 2 teaspoons freshly squeezed lemon juice, divided

¾ cup finely chopped fresh basil, divided, plus whole basil for garnish

Sea salt and freshly ground black pepper

½ cup (1 stick) unsalted butter

2 garlic cloves, minced

2 balls (each 8 ounces) burrata

Extra-virgin olive oil

Making ravioli is a fun project (perfect date night activity), and it's hard to argue with the results—perfect pasta pillows filled with a rich, creamy combination of herbed fresh ricotta and Parmesan cheese and dressed simply with garlicky butter, burrata, and basil. You could, however, serve these ravioli topped with tomato sauce (page 92), or a cream-based sauce (page 95). If you want to break up the process, make the pasta dough one day, and then roll, fill, and cook the ravioli the next. I love to serve these ravioli with a Caesar salad (page 47) or a simple salad of arugula, olive oil, lemon, and Parmesan cheese.

Using the instructions on page 75, roll your fresh pasta dough into sheets, about 1/16 inch thick. Cover with a kitchen towel so the dough doesn't dry out while you prepare the filling.

In a medium bowl, combine the ricotta, ½ cup of the Parmesan, lemon zest, 2 teaspoons of the lemon juice, and ¼ cup of the finely chopped basil. Season with salt and pepper to taste.

Working with one pasta sheet at a time, arrange the pasta sheet on your work surface with a long side facing you. On the bottom half of the dough, place rounded teaspoons of filling in a row, spacing them 1 inch apart, over half of the pasta sheet. Fold the top half of the sheet over the bottom, enclosing the filling and pressing out any air bubbles. Press the edges of the dough together to seal. Using a pasta cutter or pizza wheel, cut each ravioli into a square. Repeat with the remaining pasta and filling.

Bring a large pot of salted water to a boil over high heat.

Melt the butter in a large, high-sided skillet over medium heat. Cook until the butter is lightly browned and smells nutty, skimming off the foam as necessary, about 5 to 7 minutes. Add the garlic, the remaining 1 tablespoon of the lemon juice, the remaining ½ cup of the finely chopped basil, and several cracks of pepper and cook, stirring, until the garlic is fragrant, 2 minutes. Set aside.

Add the ravioli to the boiling water (in batches, if necessary), and cook until they float and are firm to the touch, about 2 to 3 minutes. The ravioli cook very quickly, so keep a close eye on them to avoid overcooking.

Using a slotted spoon or spider, transfer your ravioli directly from the boiling water to the skillet with the butter sauce (and do not drain the pasta water). When all of the ravioli have been added to the butter sauce, add about ¼ cup of the pasta water and the remaining ¼ cup of the Parmesan cheese. Cook over low heat, gently tossing the ravioli until it is coated in the butter sauce, the Parmesan has melted, and the skillet sauce is creamy and emulsified, about 2 minutes Add additional pasta water as needed.

Transfer the pasta to individual serving dishes, and top each serving with some of the burrata. Drizzle the burrata with the olive oil and season with salt and pepper. Garnish with the basil and serve.

Pappardelle with Creamy Mushrooms

6 tablespoons unsalted butter, divided

2 tablespoons extra-virgin olive oil, divided

1 small yellow onion, finely chopped

Sea salt

4 garlic cloves, minced

¼ cup dry white wine

1 pound chanterelle mushrooms

1½ cups heavy (35%) cream

Zest of 1 lemon

½ cup Parmesan cheese, plus more for serving

Freshly ground black pepper

1 pound pappardelle pasta

2 cups baby spinach

¼ cup finely chopped fresh flat-leaf parsley

This pasta is really about the marriage of a handful of delicious things: meaty yet mild chanterelle mushrooms, luscious heavy cream, and Parmesan cheese, which come together in a simple sauce that cloaks the delicate pappardelle. The baby spinach stirred in at the end wilts into silky ribbons. If you can't find chanterelle mushrooms (which are seasonal), worry not! You can certainly substitute cremini mushrooms; simply remove the stems and quarter the caps and you're good to go.

Bring a large stockpot of salted water to a boil.

Heat 3 tablespoons of the butter and 1 tablespoon of the olive oil in a large skillet over medium heat until the butter has melted. Add the onion, season with a pinch of salt, and cook, stirring often, until softened and translucent, about 4 to 5 minutes.

Add the garlic and cook for 30 seconds, and then pour in the wine. Let the wine bubble and simmer away until reduced by half, about 2 minutes. Add the remaining 3 tablespoons of the butter, the remaining 1 tablespoon of the olive oil, and the mushrooms. Cook, stirring often, until the mushrooms have started to turn golden brown, about 8 minutes. Stir in the cream, lemon zest, and Parmesan, and reduce the heat to medium-low. Let the sauce bubble away until thickened, about 5 to 6 minutes, and season to taste with salt and pepper.

While the sauce is simmering, cook the noodles according to the package directions until al dente.

Stir the spinach into the sauce and cook for about 30 seconds, and then add the parsley. Drain the pasta, reserving ½ cup of pasta water, and add both to the skillet with the sauce, stirring to coat the noodles with the sauce. Taste, then adjust seasoning as necessary. Serve right away, with additional Parmesan alongside.

Smoked Bolognese

¼ cup extra-virgin olive oil

½ teaspoon red pepper flakes

1 large white onion, diced

2 large carrots, peeled and diced

3 celery stalks, diced

Sea salt

4 garlic cloves

1 tablespoon minced fresh rosemary

1 tablespoon minced fresh thyme

1 tablespoon minced basil stems

1½ tablespoons tomato paste

1½ pounds ground beef (80/20)

1½ pounds ground Italian sausage, casings removed

2 cups dry red wine

1 jar (28 ounces) passata (tomato purée)

3 cups beef stock

1 tablespoon balsamic vinegar

1 Parmesan rind (optional)

Zest of 1 lemon

1 cup grated Parmesan cheese

½ cup finely chopped fresh basil

Freshly ground black pepper

A Maritime winter is long, dark, and cold. It's beautiful, particularly if you're the kind of soul that enjoys snow-packed . . . everything. But for me, my soul longs for palm trees, beaches, and rainbow-colored drinks with tiny umbrellas. Thankfully, food has an incredible way of warming your soul even on the darkest of days. While I wait for spring to arrive, I do the sort of low, slow cooking that's suited to the season, like this stick-to-your-ribs braised meat sauce. Cooked in a pellet grill or smoker, the sauce becomes imbued with smoky flavor, but of course it can be made in an oven. I make this recipe often as it freezes perfectly. Simply divide into your preferred servings, freeze, and weeknight meals become a breeze. Serve the sauce tossed with pasta, spooned over polenta, or on its own with a hunk of crusty bread.

Preheat the oven, pellet grill, or smoker to 325°F.

Heat the olive oil a large Dutch oven or high-sided, heavy-bottomed pot over medium heat until the oil is shimmering. Carefully add the red pepper flakes and cook, stirring, for 30 seconds. Add the onion, carrot, and celery, season with a pinch of salt, and cook until the vegetables are softened and translucent, about 6 to 8 minutes.

Add the garlic, rosemary, thyme, and basil stems, and cook for 30 seconds. Stir in the tomato paste and cook for 1 minute, stirring constantly. Add the ground beef and sausage, and season with a pinch of salt. Use a wooden spoon to break up the meat and cook, stirring, until it begins to brown, 6 to 8 minutes. Add the red wine, bring to a simmer, and simmer until reduced by half, about 10 minutes.

Add the passata, stock, balsamic, Parmesan rind (if using), and lemon zest, and return to a simmer. Transfer to your oven, grill, or smoker and cook, stirring every 30 minutes or so, until the liquid has reduced and the sauce is thick and glossy, about 3 hours.

To finish, stir in the Parmesan and chopped basil and season to taste with salt and pepper. To freeze the Bolognese, let cool to room temperature, transfer to plastic freezer storage bags, and stack flat in your freezer for up to 3 months.

Spicy Pasta alla Norma

2 medium eggplants, cut into ½-inch cubes

Sea salt

2 to 4 tablespoons extra-virgin olive oil

1 pound hot Italian sausage, casing removed and shaped into small meatballs

4 garlic cloves, minced

1 tablespoon finely chopped fresh basil stems

½ teaspoon red pepper flakes

1 tablespoon capers

1 tablespoon tomato paste

1 teaspoon dried oregano

1 tablespoon red wine vinegar

1 tablespoon lemon zest

1 can (28 ounces) crushed tomatoes

Freshly ground black pepper

1 pound dried casarecce pasta

½ cup finely chopped fresh basil

½ cup pecorino Romano cheese, plus more for serving

Like so many of us, I travel to eat. Often while traveling, I try a new dish that I immediately know I have to re-create when back in my home kitchen. Enter pasta alla Norma. This is my riff on a traditional Sicilian pasta named after the opera *Norma*, written by Vincent Bellini, a native of the ancient port city Catania. While this pasta is typically vegetarian, with lots of robust flavor contributed by the capers and garlic, I take mine up a notch with hot Italian sausage. If you prefer a vegetarian pasta, just omit the sausage. Easy-peasy. Finally, perfectly salty sheep's milk pecorino Romano is the necessary finishing touch to take this dish into the stratosphere.

Place a colander in the sink, add the eggplant, sprinkle generously with salt, and toss. Let sit for 20 minutes, rinse well, and pat dry with paper towel. Set aside.

Bring a large pot of salted water to a rolling boil.

Heat 2 tablespoons of the olive oil in a large, high-sided skillet over medium heat. When the oil is hot, add the sausage meatballs and cook, turning the meatballs with a spoon, until golden on all sides, about 5 minutes (the meatballs will not be cooked through but will finish cooking in the sauce). With a slotted spoon, transfer the meatballs to a plate, leaving the fat in the skillet.

Working in batches, add some of the eggplant to the skillet and fry, stirring every few minutes, until golden brown on all sides, about 5 to 8 minutes. Transfer to a plate and repeat until all of the eggplant has been fried, adding some of the remaining oil to the skillet if necessary.

When all of the eggplant has been fried, add the garlic, basil stems, and red pepper flakes to the skillet. Cook for 1 minute, stirring often. Stir in the capers, tomato paste, and oregano and cook 1 more minute. Add the vinegar, lemon zest, and tomatoes, and season with a nice pinch of salt and pepper. Return the sausage meatballs and eggplant to the skillet, bring to a simmer, and cook until thick and glossy, about 20 minutes.

While the sauce is simmering, cook the pasta according to package directions until al dente. Drain, reserving ½ cup of the pasta water, and return the pasta to the pot. Add the sauce mixture to the pasta, along with the reserved pasta water, chopped basil, and pecorino. Stir vigorously to coat the pasta with the sauce. Season to taste with salt and pepper, and serve immediately.

Grilled Shrimp with Tomato-y Orzo and Salsa Verde

For the shrimp

1½ pounds shell-on large shrimp, deveined

2 tablespoons extra-virgin olive oil

1 tablespoon lemon zest

1 garlic clove, minced

⅛ teaspoon crushed red pepper flakes

For the salsa verde

2 tablespoons capers

2 oil-packed anchovy fillets

2 garlic cloves, minced

1 cup fresh flat-leaf parsley

½ cup fresh basil

Zest of 1 lemon

5 tablespoons extra-virgin olive oil

Sea salt

For the orzo

2 tablespoons extra-virgin olive oil

1 medium yellow onion, finely chopped

½ cup finely diced fennel, fronds reserved

1 tablespoon minced fresh basil stems

2 garlic cloves, minced

1 tablespoon tomato paste

¼ cup dry white wine

1 cup orzo

3 cups vegetable or porcini stock, homemade (page 109) or store-bought

1 cup passata (tomato purée)

Zest of 1 lemon

Sea salt and freshly ground black pepper

This recipe is inspired by a grilled lobster and orzo dish I had in Tulum, a culinary and vacation haven in Mexico's Yucatan province. I ordered it off the menu, and the chef realized he'd run out of lobster—so he ran to the dock to grab one for me. Talk about fresh! Here, I've swapped lobster for shrimp, and I've added an herbaceous salsa verde to brighten the dish. The combination of smoky charred shrimp, garlicky tomato orzo, and lively salsa verde makes this dish perfect for enjoying on a patio on a warm summer's evening with a chilled bottle of your favorite crisp white wine. You can make the salsa verde a few hours ahead, but if you're pressed for time, you could substitute several heaping tablespoons of store-bought basil pesto.

Prepare the Shrimp: In a bowl, toss to combine the shrimp, olive oil, lemon zest, garlic, and red pepper flakes. Place in the fridge and marinate for 20 minutes.

Make the Salsa Verde: In a food processor, combine the capers, anchovies, garlic, parsley, basil, and lemon zest, and pulse until finely chopped and a paste begins to form. In a slow and steady stream, drizzle in the olive oil until thickened and emulsified. Season to taste with salt.

Prepare a grill for direct, medium-high heat grilling (see Notes on Grilling, page 187).

Prepare the Orzo: Heat the olive oil in a large, high-sided skillet over medium heat until the oil is shimmering. Carefully add the onion, fennel, and basil stems, and cook until the vegetables are softened, 6 to 8 minutes. Stir in the garlic and tomato paste, and cook, stirring often, for 2 minutes. Add the white wine and cook, stirring often, until almost entirely evaporated. Add the orzo, stock, passata, and lemon zest, and season with a good pinch each of salt and pepper. Stir to combine and bring to a boil. Cook, stirring often, for 8 to 10 minutes, or until the orzo is cooked through with an al dente bite. Taste and adjust the seasoning as necessary.

Lay the shrimp on the grill and grill for 2 to 3 minutes per side, or until the shrimp are bright pink and cooked through and the shells are crispy and golden.

Divide the orzo into bowls. Top each serving with some of the grilled shrimp and a few spoonfuls of salsa verde. Serve with the remaining salsa verde alongside.

Pappardelle with Mussels, Shrimp, and Chorizo

2 tablespoons extra-virgin olive oil

½ pound fresh chorizo, casings removed

½ medium red onion, diced

Sea salt

4 garlic cloves, minced

2 tablespoons tomato paste

1½ pounds large shrimp, shelled and deveined

1 pound pappardelle pasta

1 cup dry white wine

1 tablespoon lemon zest

1 pound mussels, scrubbed and debearded

1 tablespoon minced fresh tarragon

Juice of ½ lemon

Freshly ground black pepper

2 tablespoons minced fresh flat-leaf parsley

A seafood lover's dream! Chockablock full of seaside goodness, this is my ideal summertime pasta. It's satisfying but light, and I love the combination of the spicy chorizo with the abundant shellfish. If you'd like, you can replace some (or all) of the mussels with small clams, depending on what's available at your local fishmonger. Choose a dry white wine you like to drink, and pour yourself a glass (or two) while you make this pasta. The best way to cook.

Bring a large stockpot of salted water to a boil.

Heat the olive oil in a large, high-sided skillet over medium heat until the oil is shimmering (but not smoking). Carefully add the chorizo and cook, breaking up the chunks with a wooden spoon, until golden and cooked through, about 6 minutes. Remove with a slotted spoon, leaving the excess oil in the skillet.

Add the onion, season with a pinch of salt, and cook, stirring, until softened and translucent, about 4 to 5 minutes. Add the garlic and cook, stirring, for 30 seconds, keeping a close watch so that it doesn't burn. Stir in the tomato paste and cook for 1 minute. Add the shrimp, season with salt, and cook for 1 minute. Remove the skillet from the heat.

Add the pasta to the boiling water and cook according to the package directions until al dente. Drain, reserving 1 cup of the pasta water, and return the pasta to the pot.

Return the skillet with the shrimp to medium heat and add the wine, reserved pasta water, lemon zest, and mussels. Cover and cook until the mussels are fully opened, about 5 minutes (discard any mussels that do not open). Pour the shrimp and mussel mixture into the pot with the pasta, add the chorizo and tarragon, and toss to combine. Squeeze the lemon juice over. Season to taste with additional salt and pepper. Transfer to a serving platter or individual plates, and sprinkle with the parsley.

Cacio e Pepe

1 tablespoon whole black peppercorns, plus more freshly ground black pepper, for serving

2 teaspoons sea salt

¾ pound spaghetti, bucatini, linguine, or other long pasta

2½ cups finely grated pecorino Romano, at room temperature, plus more for serving

Extra-virgin olive oil, for drizzling

The first time I visited Rome, I ate cacio e pepe at a tiny restaurant after an AS Roma soccer match. Even though it was 1 a.m., the server made it tableside, tossing together the few ingredients until it coalesced, each noodle coated in a creamy sauce that—shockingly—includes no cream at all. Cacio e pepe exemplifies the North Star that guides Italian cuisine and has been my constant inspiration since I first visited the Bel Paese: a few ingredients, cooked well, become more than the sum of their parts. This recipe also demonstrates the power of the starchy pasta cooking water, which is a key ingredient, emulsifying with the pecorino Romano to make a sauce that cloaks the pasta. Don't be tempted to substitute another cheese for the salty sheep's milk pecorino Romano—it makes the dish. And if you've never made cacio e pepe before, welcome to your new favorite date-night and late-night dish.

Grab your trusty mortar and pestle or spice grinder, and bash (or grind) the peppercorns until finely ground.

Fill a stockpot with 2 quarts of water, add the salt, and bring to a rapid boil. (You're using less water than normal to boil the pasta so that the water becomes very starchy; that starchy pasta cooking liquid is key to the consistency of the sauce.)

Add the pasta to the boiling water. You're going to intentionally undercook the pasta and finish cooking it in the sauce. If the package directions instruct you to cook the pasta for 10 minutes, remove the pasta around 6 minutes; it should be very al dente. Reserve the pasta cooking water.

Just before the pasta is done, heat a skillet over medium-low heat and add the ground peppercorns. Toast, stirring, until fragrant, about 30 seconds. Add 1 cup of the pasta cooking water and bring to a simmer.

Put the pecorino in a large bowl and mix with just enough hot pasta water to form a paste.

Using tongs, transfer the pasta directly to the skillet and continue cooking, stirring often and adding pasta water as necessary, until the pasta is cooked through but toothsome, and the sauce looks creamy, about 2 to 3 minutes.

Add the pasta and any liquid to the bowl of cheese and stir vigorously, adding a bit more pasta water if necessary, until the sauce is thick, creamy, and emulsified and cloaks the noodles.

Divide among four warmed bowls. Spoon over any sauce remaining in the bowl, and garnish each serving with a bit of freshly ground black pepper, grated pecorino Romano, and a drizzle of olive oil. Serve immediately. Mamma mia!

Rigatoni alla Carbonara

1 pound rigatoni

3 tablespoons extra-virgin olive oil, divided

¼ pound diced guanciale or pancetta

6 large egg yolks

2 large eggs

¼ cup finely grated Parmesan cheese, plus more for serving

¼ cup finely grated pecorino Romano

2 teaspoons freshly ground black pepper, plus more for serving

Sea salt

Whenever I wish I were in Italy instead of my Canadian kitchen, this is the pasta dish I like to make. For me, it's unquestionably the ultimate Italian comfort food. The name comes from the word *carbonaro*, or coal-burner, and legend has it the recipe was developed to feed hungry working men simply but heartily. Though you can use a variety of pasta shapes for carbonara, including spaghetti, I am partial to rigatoni—the noodles trap the sauce and meaty bits. Traditionally, carbonara is made with guanciale (cured pork cheeks), common in Italy but harder to find in North America. You might be able to get them at an Italian grocer or butcher shop, if you have one near you. If not, substitute with pancetta—it will be just as good. Go with quality ingredients for this dish, though. Get real Parmesan cheese and pecorino Romano cheese, and use the best-quality farm-fresh eggs.

Bring a large pot of salted water to a rapid boil, add the rigatoni, and cook the pasta according to the package directions until al dente. Reserve the pasta water.

While the water heats and the pasta cooks, heat 2 tablespoons of the olive oil in a large, high-sided skillet over medium heat until the oil is shimmering. Carefully add the guanciale and cook, stirring often, until the fat has rendered and the guanciale is crisp, about 6 to 8 minutes. Remove the skillet from the heat.

In a large, metal, heatproof bowl, whisk together the egg yolks, whole eggs, Parmesan, pecorino, and black pepper.

Return the skillet with the guanciale to medium-low heat. Using tongs, transfer the cooked pasta to the skillet and toss with your crispy guanciale and fat from the skillet. Remove from the heat, add the remaining 1 tablespoon olive oil, and cool for a moment or two. Return the pasta water back to a boil.

Add the rigatoni, guanciale, and fat to the egg mixture, along with ½ cup of the pasta cooking water. Toss well. Place the bowl over the pot of boiling water, making sure that the bottom of the bowl doesn't touch the water itself (if you need to, you can pour out some of the boiling water). Cook, tossing with tongs, until the sauce thickens and becomes creamy, with a super silky consistency. Remove from the heat, taste, and season with salt if necessary.

Divide the rigatoni between four warmed serving bowls. Top each with extra Parmesan and pepper, and serve immediately.

My Go-To Tomato Sauce

¼ cup extra-virgin olive oil

½ white onion, finely chopped

Sea salt

6 garlic cloves, minced

2 tablespoons minced fresh basil stems

½ teaspoon red pepper flakes

2 teaspoons dried oregano

2 tablespoons tomato paste

1 jar (28 ounces) passata (tomato purée)

Zest of ½ lemon

Freshly ground black pepper

1 tablespoon freshly squeezed lemon juice

¼ cup finely grated Parmesan cheese

¼ cup minced fresh basil

Having a banging tomato sauce in your arsenal is essential and works for an abundance of recipes. Pastas, braised chicken, fish, or even baked feta—that tomato sauce is going to come in handy! I love tomato-based sauces so much, in fact, that there are two included in this book. The bright and fresh marinara on page 31 and this recipe, best used when you're looking to jack that flavor up to 11. Sure, you can buy decent tomato sauce at the grocery store. But making your own is super simple, and it tastes much fresher and more delicious than anything out of a jar. If you want, double this recipe like I often do and freeze half for a rainy day.

Heat the olive oil in a large saucepan over medium heat until the oil is shimmering. Carefully add the onion, season with a pinch of salt, and cook, stirring occasionally, until softened and translucent, 6 to 7 minutes.

Add the garlic, basil stems, red pepper flakes, oregano, and tomato paste. Cook for 45 seconds, and then pour in the passata. Add the lemon zest, season with salt and pepper, and bring to a simmer. Cook for 10 to 12 minutes, until thickened and bubbly. Squeeze in the lemon juice, and then remove from the heat and stir in the Parmesan and basil. Season to taste with additional salt and pepper. To store, cool to room temperature, and refrigerate in an airtight container for up to 5 days, or transfer to plastic freezer bags and freeze for up to 6 months.

Roasted Cauliflower Rigatoni with Pangrattato

1 head garlic

¼ cup extra-virgin olive oil, divided

Sea salt and freshly ground black pepper

1 large head of cauliflower, separated into florets

2 tablespoons capers, drained

1 pound rigatoni

1 tablespoon unsalted butter

½ teaspoon crushed red pepper flakes

1¾ cups heavy (35%) cream

1 tablespoon lemon zest

½ cup freshly grated Parmesan cheese, plus more for serving

Juice of ½ lemon

¼ cup minced fresh flat-leaf parsley

1 batch Pangrattato (see page 14)

The humble cauliflower deserves much more love. It's inexpensive, readily available, and delicious grilled, roasted, puréed, or even raw. Oh, and it's healthy to boot. Bonus! I love pastas that are perfect for a quick weeknight meal at home and that even the fussiest of eaters will love. To add extra dimension to this simple and decadent cream sauce–based pasta, I roast the cauliflower and capers until golden and crispy, add a whole head of roasted garlic, and season the sauce with red pepper flakes and lemon. Last, I love to add a buttery and cheesy breadcrumb topping that gives this pasta a beautiful texture when served.

Preheat the oven (or grill) to 425°F and line a large baking sheet with parchment paper.

Cut about ¼ inch off the top of the head of garlic, exposing the cloves but leaving the root intact. Drizzle the exposed cloves with olive oil, and season with salt and pepper. Wrap in foil and roast for 30 to 40 minutes, or until the cloves are golden and super soft. Let rest until cool enough to handle, squeeze the cloves onto a cutting board, and mash into a paste. Roasted garlic is heaven on earth.

Meanwhile, arrange the cauliflower on the prepared baking sheet. Toss with the capers and 2 tablespoons of the olive oil, and season well with salt and pepper. Roast, stirring occasionally, until the cauliflower is golden and starting to crisp, about 30 to 35 minutes.

Bring a large pot of salted water to a rapid boil over high heat. Add the rigatoni and cook according to the package directions until al dente.

Meanwhile, heat the remaining 2 tablespoons of the olive oil and the butter in a large skillet over medium heat. When the butter has melted, add the red pepper flakes and cook for 1 minute. Add the roasted garlic paste, heavy cream, and lemon zest, and season with salt and pepper. Bring the sauce to a gentle simmer, and let it bubble away and reduce while your pasta cooks. Just before adding your cooked pasta to the sauce, sprinkle in the Parmesan and stir until melted.

Drain the pasta, reserving ¼ cup of the pasta cooking water. Add the pasta to the skillet with the sauce, along with the reserved pasta water and lemon juice, and toss well. Add the cauliflower mixture and parsley, and toss well to combine. Transfer to individual dishes. Evenly top each serving with some of the pangrattato, a sprinkle of Parmesan, and a bit of pepper. Serve right away.

Gnudi with Tomato Sauce and Herbed Vinaigrette

4 cups whole-milk ricotta cheese, drained

½ cup finely grated Parmesan cheese, plus more for serving

½ cup finely grated pecorino Romano

2 large free-range eggs

Zest of 1 lemon

Sea salt and freshly ground black pepper

2 cups all-purpose flour, divided

1 batch My Go-To Tomato Sauce (page 92) or 3 cups store-bought marinara sauce

1 batch Herbed Vinaigrette (page 249)

¼ cup chopped fresh basil

Gnudi: fun to say, and even more fun to make. The success of this recipe relies on two things: the quality of the ricotta cheese and how gently you handle the tender, delicate dough. Look for the thickest whole-milk ricotta you can find, and don't skip the step of draining it in a fine-mesh sieve to remove excess moisture. Form the gnudi gently, and let chill for the full 30 minutes before boiling, which will prevent them from falling apart. I like to serve the gnudi with marinara and herbed vinaigrette, but you could toss them with only butter and Parmesan, or basil pesto (page 124).

Place your ricotta in a fine-mesh sieve set over a medium bowl, and let drain to remove excess moisture.

Place the Parmesan and pecorino in a large bowl. Mix in the ricotta, eggs, and lemon zest. Season well with salt and pepper. Add 1 cup of the flour and stir until just combined.

Dust a rimmed baking sheet with ½ cup of the flour, spreading it in an even layer. Divide and very gently shape your gnudi into small 1½-inch golf balls. *Gently* place them onto the prepared baking sheet. When all of the gnudi have been formed, dust with the remaining ½ cup flour, and transfer to the refrigerator and chill for 30 minutes. Don't skip this step! It's essential to ensure your gnudi don't fall apart in the water.

Bring a large pot of salted water to a rapid boil. Pour your tomato sauce into a small saucepan and warm over medium-low heat until gently bubbling away.

Working in batches, very gently drop half of your gnudi into the boiling water, 1 or 2 at a time, taking care not to add too much excess flour to the water. Cook until the gnudi float and become firm to the touch, about 3 to 5 minutes. With a slotted spoon, transfer to a large bowl, and repeat with the remaining gnudi.

When all of the gnudi have been cooked, add the tomato sauce to the bowl with the gnudi. Using a rubber spatula, gently toss to coat the gnudi with sauce. Divide among plates. Top each serving with a drizzle of vinaigrette, some of the chopped basil, and some pepper.

Baked Ziti with Grilled Chicken, Spinach, and Crème Fraîche

3 large boneless, skinless chicken breasts, about 1½ pounds

¾ cup plus 2 tablespoons extra-virgin olive oil, divided

¼ cup red wine vinegar

7 garlic cloves, minced, divided

1½ teaspoons dried oregano

1 teaspoon dried basil

1½ teaspoons crushed red pepper flakes, divided

1 tablespoon lemon zest

Juice of ½ lemon

Sea salt and freshly ground black pepper

1 pound ziti (you could also substitute penne or rigatoni)

¼ cup unsalted butter

6 tablespoons all-purpose flour

3 cups whole milk

1 cup crème fraîche

1⅓ cups grated Parmesan cheese

2½ cups grated whole-milk mozzarella cheese, divided

8 cups baby spinach, chopped

I love baked pasta dishes because they feed a crowd easily and well, and they're perfect for wintery dinner parties. Though often made with tomato sauce, this white version is enriched by a cheesy Mornay sauce that gets some tanginess from the addition of crème fraîche. Adding the grilled chicken and baby spinach makes this a complete one-pan meal. And if you want to keep this vegetarian, chicken can be omitted altogether. Entirely customizable. Totally delicious. Yes, please! Serve with your favorite salad alongside—the Caesar salad on page 47 would be delicious—and a glass (or two) of your favorite chilled white wine.

In a freezer bag (or shallow baking dish), combine the chicken breast, ¾ cup of the olive oil, the vinegar, half of the garlic, the oregano, the basil, ¾ teaspoon of the red pepper flakes, the lemon zest, and the lemon juice. Season well with salt and pepper, then turn to coat the chicken in the marinade. Cover and refrigerate at least 1 hour or up to 24 hours (the longer you can marinate it, the more delicious it will be).

Preheat a grill for direct, medium-high heat grilling (see Notes on Grilling, page 187). Lay the chicken on the grill grate and grill, flipping halfway through, until beautifully golden and charred, and an instant-read thermometer inserted into the thickest part of the meat reaches 165°F, about 10 to 12 minutes. Let rest for 5 minutes, cut into bite-size pieces, and set aside.

Preheat the oven to 400°F (or use your already preheated grill to bake your pasta—move of all moves) and bring a large pot of salted water to a rapid boil. Brush a 9 x 13-inch baking dish with olive oil.

Cook the ziti according to the package directions until al dente, drain, and transfer to a large bowl.

While the pasta cooks, heat the remaining 2 tablespoons of the olive oil and the butter in a large saucepan over medium heat. When the butter is melted, add the remaining ¾ teaspoon of the red pepper flakes and the remaining garlic. Cook, stirring, for 45 seconds, keeping a close watch so that the garlic doesn't burn. Whisk in the flour and cook until bubbling, golden, and fragrant, 1 to 2 minutes. In a slow and steady stream, whisk in the milk until smooth. Bring to a gentle simmer and cook until thickened, 4 to 5 minutes. Season to taste with a pinch of salt and pepper, and whisk in the crème fraiche. Whisk in the Parmesan and 1½ cups of the mozzarella, a small handful at a time, whisking until melted and completely incorporated. Stir in the spinach, and set aside.

recipe continues

Pour the sauce mixture into the bowl with the ziti, add the chopped grilled chicken, and mix well to combine. Transfer to the prepared baking dish. Top with the remaining 1 cup of the mozzarella cheese and several cracks of black pepper. Bake until golden, melted, and slightly crisp, and your kitchen smells like heaven, about 25 to 30 minutes.

Cooking Note: *If you, like me, live in a snowy wonderland for several months of the year, and when a nor'easter visits town you typically avoid lighting the grill, you can roast the chicken. Preheat the oven to 425°F, and set an oven-safe skillet over medium-high heat. Sauté the chicken in the skillet for 1 minute. Flip and roast in the oven until cooked through and an instant-read thermometer inserted into the thickest part of the meat reaches 165°F, about 12 to 14 minutes. Let rest for 5 minutes, cut into bite-size pieces, and set aside. If you're pressed for time, you could substitute chopped rotisserie chicken meat for the grilled chicken—you'll need about 3 cups of the chopped meat.*

Sunday Lunch Lasagna

7 tablespoons unsalted butter

6 tablespoons all-purpose flour

3 garlic cloves, minced

3½ cups whole milk

1 tablespoon lemon zest

Pinch of nutmeg

1¼ cups finely grated Parmesan cheese, divided

Sea salt and freshly ground black pepper

1 batch Smoked Bolognese (page 80)

1 pound fresh lasagna sheets, homemade (page 75) or store-bought

4 cups grated fresh mozzarella cheese (about 1 pound)

½ cup chopped fresh basil, plus more for garnish

Extra-virgin olive oil, for drizzling

From before I can even remember, I've loved lasagna. It's the height of crowd-pleasing comfort food. It can be luxurious and quite high-end or rustic and served family-style, but either way it's just . . . perfect. Making a lasagna is a bit of a commitment, particularly if you make the pasta from scratch (page 75) along with the homemade Bolognese and béchamel. But! It's the kind of commitment that gives you a beautiful sense of accomplishment. Highly recommended. To make life a little more chill, you can break the work up over a few days, making the components one day and assembling and baking it the next. And, of course, lasagna improves upon sitting, so you can always bake it the day before you plan to serve it. Or you can prepare the lasagna and freeze it, unbaked, for a rainy day; you don't need to thaw it before baking, but add 15 minutes to the baking time.

Melt the butter in a large saucepan over medium heat. When the butter has melted, whisk in the flour and cook, whisking until the flour is nutty, golden, and fragrant, 2 to 3 minutes. Add the garlic and cook for 45 seconds. Whisk in 1 cup of the milk in a slow and steady stream until smooth and thick. Continue whisking in the milk until it has all been added and the sauce is smooth. Let the sauce bubble, stirring occasionally, until it thickens and coats the back of a wooden spoon, 6 to 7 minutes. Stir in the lemon zest, nutmeg, and 1 cup of the Parmesan. Season to taste with salt and pepper.

Preheat the oven to 350°F.

Spread 1 cup of the Bolognese on the bottom of a 9 x 13-inch baking dish. Cover with lasagna sheets (trim the sheets as needed to fit). Spoon 2 cups of the Bolognese sauce over the noodles and spread evenly. Spread 1 cup of béchamel over the Bolognese sauce, and sprinkle on 1½ cups of the mozzarella cheese in an even layer, followed by 2 tablespoons of chopped basil. Repeat the layering until you have used all of the noodles, Bolognese, béchamel, mozzarella, and basil. Sprinkle the top with the remaining ¼ cup of the Parmesan, drizzle with a bit of olive oil, and sprinkle with pepper.

Bake the lasagna until bubbling and golden, about 40 to 45 minutes. Let stand for at least 10 minutes, and then cut into squares and serve. Garnish each serving with fresh basil.

Plant
Powered
Vegetable-Forward Mains

I was a child of the eighties (cool, I feel old now), growing up in Canada, so I can remember a time when vegetarian food was still kind of fringe: a lot of brown rice, a few veggie burgers, sad three-ingredient salads, and a lot of sundried tomatoes. (Oh, and hockey hair, Walkmans, and neon everything.) My mom has been a steadfast vegetarian since the mid-eighties, so plant-based eating, albeit not a great representation of said plants, has been a part of my life since I was a kid. In the ensuing thirty years, a lot has happened. In Canada and the United States, vegetables moved from the side of the plate to the center, and chefs started celebrating them as the miracles they are. Farmer's markets proliferated; vegetarian and even vegan cooking has become mainstream. And I am here for it!

Elsewhere in the world, as I discovered when I started traveling, vegetarian food is neither fringe nor fad; it's simply a flavor-forward, planet-positive, healthful, and budget-friendly way of feeding yourself. I became inspired. And while I still eat meat, I now happily and frequently cook vegetarian or vegetable-centric meals. Beyond the real need to cut down on meat consumption for the health of both our planet and ourselves, vegetables are, as far as I'm concerned, inspiring to work with. Vegetables and plant-based eating are the future and a delicious one at that. This chapter includes some of my favorite vegetable-forward main courses. There are a handful of soups for each season, tofu bowls, a sheet-pan supper for an easy weeknight dinner, and yes, because I couldn't help myself, my version of a burger—a satisfying, spiced black bean and grain patty that will delight omnivores and vegetarians alike.

Porcini Mushroom Stock

4½ quarts water, divided

4 ounces dried porcini mushrooms

2 tablespoons extra-virgin olive oil

2 tablespoons unsalted butter

1 large yellow onion, roughly chopped

1 leek, trimmed, white and light green parts chopped

3 large carrots, roughly chopped

2 celery stalks, roughly chopped

2 parsnips, roughly chopped

2 cups chopped cremini mushrooms (about 8 ounces)

1 head garlic, halved

1 teaspoon whole black peppercorns

6 fresh parsley sprigs

3 fresh thyme sprigs

3 fresh rosemary sprigs

2 bay leaves

1 lemon, halved

Porcini stock is like a secret weapon of deliciousness. Once you start making it, I guarantee it will be awarded a permanent home in your culinary bag of tricks. Made-from-scratch stock is one of those staples that really takes your food to the next level, and it's a fantastic way to use up odds and ends from vegetables that might otherwise end up in the bin, making our kitchens more sustainable and waste-free. And, as you'll notice throughout this book, once you start cooking, you'll be using a lot of stock. A lot. You can use it as the base for soup, of course, but when I've got it, it tends to find its way into all sorts of dishes, from the Grilled Shrimp with Tomato-y Orzo and Salsa Verde (page 84) to the Whiskey Peppercorn Sauce on (page 245).

Bring 4 cups of water to a rapid boil. Place the porcini mushrooms in a heatproof bowl, pour over the boiling water, and let stand for 20 minutes. Strain through a fine-mesh sieve, reserving the liquid and mushrooms separately.

Heat the olive oil and butter in a large stockpot over medium heat. When the butter has melted, add the onion and cook, stirring occasionally, until softened, translucent, and starting to caramelize, about 20 to 25 minutes. Stir in the leeks, carrots, celery, parsnips, cremini mushrooms, and reserved porcini mushrooms. Cook until the vegetables are softened and fragrant, about 20 minutes.

Pour in the reserved mushroom soaking liquid and the remaining 3½ quarts water. Add the garlic, peppercorns, parsley, thyme, rosemary, bay leaves, and lemon halves. Bring to a boil, reduce the heat to medium-low, and let simmer for 1 hour.

Strain the stock through a fine-mesh sieve set over a large bowl or pot, using the back of a spoon to press down on the vegetables to make sure you squeeze out every last drop of porcini-kissed goodness. Cool, and transfer to airtight containers. Store in the refrigerator for up to 3 days or in the freezer for up to 6 months.

Creamy Broccoli Soup with Cheddar-Chive Biscuits

For the biscuits

3 cups all-purpose flour

2 tablespoons sugar

2 teaspoons baking powder

¾ teaspoon baking soda

½ teaspoon sea salt, plus more for sprinkling

½ cup (1 stick) butter, cut into small cubes and frozen

1¼ cups grated aged cheddar cheese, divided

4 garlic cloves, minced to a paste

1 tablespoon lemon zest

3 tablespoons minced fresh chives

¾ cup cold buttermilk

1 large egg

For the soup

2 tablespoons extra-virgin olive oil

3 tablespoons unsalted butter

1 large white onion, diced

1 large carrot, peeled and diced

Sea salt

2 garlic cloves, minced

⅓ cup all-purpose flour

3½ cups vegetable or porcini stock, homemade (page 109) or store-bought

4 cups roughly chopped broccoli florets

½ teaspoon smoked paprika

¼ teaspoon ground cayenne

Freshly ground black pepper

2 cups heavy (35%) cream, plus more for drizzling

2 cups grated aged cheddar cheese

1 tablespoon minced fresh chives

For me, the best meals are made up of those nostalgic, comforting dishes that remind you of the best times in life. This soup is my childhood in a bowl, albeit slightly modernized and a tad more flavor-packed. Super cheesy and creamy heart-warming broccoli soup with flaky, buttery cheddar-chive biscuits. Talk about happiness in a bite! The biscuit recipe makes more than you might eat alongside the soup, but it doesn't make sense to make a smaller batch, especially because they're the perfect base for an egg and bacon breakfast sandwich the next morning.

Make the Biscuits: Preheat the oven to 375°F, and line 2 large baking sheets with parchment paper.

In a large bowl, mix together the flour, sugar, baking powder, baking soda, and salt. Add the butter and, using your fingertips, work the butter into the flour until the butter pieces are the size of small peas. Stir in 1 cup of the cheese, the garlic, lemon zest, and chives.

Make a well in the center of the flour mixture. In a separate medium bowl, whisk together the buttermilk and egg, and then pour them into the well. Gently stir the mixture until a thick dough forms.

Drop the dough in ¼-cup mounds onto the prepared baking sheets, leaving plenty of room between each drop biscuit (you should have 10 to 12 biscuits). Sprinkle the remaining ¼ cup of the cheese on top of the biscuits. Bake until puffed and lightly browned all over, about 18 to 20 minutes. Transfer to a wire rack, sprinkle with additional salt, and let cool.

Make the Soup: Heat the olive oil and butter in a large Dutch oven or large stockpot over medium heat. When the butter is melted, add the onion and carrot, season with a pinch of salt, and cook until softened, about 8 to 10 minutes. Add the garlic and cook for 1 minute. Stir in the flour, coating the vegetables well, and cook, stirring, about 1 to 2 minutes more. Add the stock, broccoli, paprika, cayenne, and a few pinches of salt and pepper. Bring to a simmer, reduce the heat to medium-low, and let the soup cook until the broccoli is cooked through, about 15 minutes. Stir in the cream and remove from the heat.

Using a hand blender (or high-powered regular blender, working in batches), pulse the soup until smooth. Return the soup to a gentle simmer. Add the cheese a handful or so at a time, stirring until melted before adding another handful. Taste and adjust the seasoning as necessary.

Divide into bowls. Top with a sprinkle of the fresh chives and an extra crack of pepper. Serve with a cheddar-chive biscuit and enter a world of bliss.

"Butter" Chickpeas

2 tablespoons extra-virgin olive oil

1 medium yellow onion, minced

4 garlic cloves, minced

1-inch piece fresh ginger, peeled and minced

2 tablespoons minced fresh cilantro stems

2 teaspoons garam masala

2 teaspoons ground cumin

1 teaspoon curry powder

1 teaspoon ground coriander

1 teaspoon smoked paprika

½ teaspoon ground turmeric

½ teaspoon cayenne pepper

1 tablespoon tomato paste

1 can (14 ounces) full-fat coconut milk

1 cup crushed tomatoes

1 cup vegetable stock

Zest of 1 lime

2 cans (each 15 ounces) chickpeas, drained and rinsed (3 cups)

Sea salt and freshly ground black pepper

2 tablespoons coconut oil

¼ cup chopped fresh cilantro, plus a few sprigs for garnish

1 lime, cut into wedges

Steamed rice or naan, for serving

Butter chicken, bless you. The first time I tried this marvelous Indian dish in all its saucy, spiced glory, I was a traveling musician working my way through Canada and we stopped at a nondescript restaurant in Montreal. It changed . . . everything. From that first bite, my idea of seasoning, depth of flavor, and just generally how delicious food could be changed forever. This is a fun riff on Indian butter chicken, except that I've swapped chickpeas for the chicken, and this version actually doesn't contain butter at all, so it's totally vegan and healthy to boot. What has remained is the luscious-spiced tomato sauce that's the hallmark of the dish. If you're not vegan, you might consider swapping the chickpeas for paneer for an equally satisfying vegetarian version.

Heat the oil in a large Dutch oven or large, heavy-bottomed pot over medium heat. Add the onions, season with a pinch of salt, and cook until softened and translucent, 4 to 5 minutes. Add the garlic, ginger, and cilantro stems, and cook for another 2 minutes. Stir in the garam masala, cumin, curry powder, coriander, paprika, turmeric, cayenne, and tomato paste and cook, stirring constantly, for 2 minutes.

Pour in the coconut milk, crushed tomatoes, stock, lime zest, and chickpeas. Season with a few good pinches each of salt and pepper, and bring to a simmer. Simmer, stirring occasionally, for about 15 to 20 minutes, or until the sauce has thickened.

Remove from the heat and stir in the coconut oil and chopped cilantro. Taste and adjust the seasoning as necessary. Divide among serving bowls. Garnish with the cilantro sprigs, and serve with lime wedges and rice or naan (or both).

Togarashi Tofu Bowls

SERVES 4

1 block (16 ounces) extra-firm tofu

¼ cup plus 2 tablespoons grapeseed oil or other neutral oil, divided

¼ cup plus 2 tablespoons soy sauce, divided

2 tablespoons pure maple syrup, divided

1 tablespoon togarashi

2 tablespoons Shaoxing rice wine or dry sherry

1 tablespoon rice vinegar

1 pound baby bok choy, trimmed and cleaned

1 tablespoon peeled and minced fresh ginger

4 garlic cloves, minced

3 green onions, minced, plus more for garnish

2 tablespoons minced fresh cilantro stems

2 bird's eye or Thai chilies, stemmed, seeded, and thinly sliced

2 tablespoons toasted sesame seeds

3 cups cooked sushi or jasmine rice

½ cup salted and roasted peanuts, chopped

½ English cucumber, thinly sliced

1 to 2 ripe avocados, sliced

2 cups mizuna, watercress, or spinach

Tofu is the great flavor absorber. Here, it gets a spice-packed boost from togarashi, a Japanese spice blend of dried chilies, sesame seeds, and dried orange zest. It's the centerpiece of these spicy rice bowls, which are tricked out with sautéed bok choy, thinly sliced cucumber, ripe avocado, and a garnish of salted peanuts. There are, of course, endless other vegetables you could add, from thinly sliced carrots to roasted sweet potato wedges or broccoli. Let your crisper, the farmer's market, and the season be your guide!

Preheat the oven to 400°F and line a baking sheet with parchment paper.

Line a plate with paper towel, and place the tofu on the paper towel. Top with more paper towel and a heavy skillet. Let stand for 15 minutes so the paper towel can absorb any excess liquid from the tofu. Cut the tofu into ½-inch cubes and transfer to a bowl. Pour in ¼ cup of the grapeseed oil, 2 tablespoons of the soy sauce, 1 tablespoon of the syrup, and the togarashi. Mix well to coat the tofu, and let stand for 20 minutes.

Arrange your tofu on the prepared baking sheet in a single layer. Bake, flipping halfway through, until crispy and golden, about 20 to 25 minutes.

In a small bowl, stir together the remaining ¼ cup of the soy sauce, the remaining 1 tablespoon of the syrup, the rice wine, and the rice vinegar.

Heat 1 tablespoon of the grapeseed oil in a large skillet over medium heat until the oil is shimmering. Carefully add the bok choy and cook, stirring, until tender, about 2 to 3 minutes. Transfer to a plate and set aside. Add the remaining 1 tablespoon of the grapeseed oil to the skillet, and then add the ginger, garlic, green onions, cilantro stems, and chilies. Cook until fragrant, about 1 to 2 minutes. Pour in the soy sauce mixture and bring to a simmer. Return the bok choy to the skillet, add the tofu to the skillet, and toss to coat well. Remove from the heat and stir in the sesame seeds.

To build your bowls, spoon some of the cooked rice into each bowl. Top with some of the tofu mixture and garnish with the peanuts, cucumber, avocado, and greens.

Black Bean Edamame Burgers

4 tablespoons grapeseed oil or other neutral oil, divided

1 medium yellow onion, finely chopped

Sea salt

½ cup cooked farro or brown rice

3 garlic cloves, minced, divided

2 cans (each 15 ounces) black beans, drained and rinsed

1½ cups panko breadcrumbs

1 cup frozen edamame, thawed

½ cup minced fresh cilantro

Zest of 1 lemon

1 tablespoon Dijon mustard

1 teaspoon ground cumin

1 teaspoon smoked paprika

Freshly ground black pepper

½ cup mayonnaise, homemade (recipe to follow) or store-bought

2 tablespoons prepared harissa paste

1 tablespoon freshly squeezed lemon juice

½ large red onion, peeled and sliced into half-moons

1 large red bell pepper, stemmed, seeded, and julienned

6 brioche burger buns, toasted

1 large tomato, thinly sliced

6 burger-size lettuce leaves

Okay, let's address some harsh truth. There are—if I'm being honest—a lot of rather terrible veggie burgers out there. But *these* are the antidote to every sad patty you may have tried over the years. Bound by a mixture of cooked farro, black beans, and panko breadcrumbs, generously spiced, and stacked on a brioche bun with a slather of harissa mayonnaise and cooked peppers and onions, this one is guaranteed to please both vegetarians and omnivores alike.

Heat 1 tablespoon of the grapeseed oil in a large skillet over medium heat until the oil is shimmering. Carefully add the yellow onion, season with a pinch of salt, and cook until softened and translucent, about 6 to 8 minutes. Set aside.

In the bowl of a food processor, combine the farro, cooked onion, ⅔ of the garlic, the black beans, panko, edamame, cilantro, lemon zest, mustard, cumin, and paprika. Season with a few pinches each of salt and pepper. Pulse until mostly smooth, with a few chunks remaining for texture. Divide and shape into 6 large burger patties, the same width as the burger buns. Transfer to a baking sheet and refrigerate for 20 minutes.

Meanwhile, in a small bowl, combine the mayonnaise, harissa, lemon juice, and a pinch of salt, and mix well. Set aside the harissa mayonnaise.

Heat 1 tablespoon of the grapeseed oil in a large skillet over medium heat until the oil is shimmering. Add the red onion and cook, stirring often, for 4 minutes. Add the bell pepper, the remaining ⅓ of the garlic, and a pinch of salt. Cook, stirring, for an additional 2 to 3 minutes, until the peppers are softened. Remove the vegetables from the skillet and set aside on a plate. When cool enough to do so, wipe the skillet clean with paper towel. Return the skillet to the burner and reduce the heat to medium.

Pour the remaining 2 tablespoons of the oil into the skillet. When the oil is hot, working in batches as necessary, fry your burgers for 4 to 5 minutes per side, until golden brown and cooked through.

Spread both sides of each bun with some of the harissa mayonnaise. Top with a burger patty, some of the sautéed vegetables, a slice of tomato, and a leaf of lettuce, and then the top bun.

AQUAFABA MAYONNAISE

Who would have ever guessed that the starchy liquid drained from a can of chickpeas would be the magical liquid that makes it possible to veganize everything from chocolate mousse to mayonnaise? When whipped, the liquid acts much the same way that egg whites behave, foaming and stabilizing. Amazing!

MAKES ABOUT 1 CUP

¼ cup aquafaba (the liquid drained from a can of chickpeas)

2 teaspoons apple cider vinegar

1 teaspoon Dijon mustard

½ teaspoon pure maple syrup

Sea salt

¾ cup grapeseed or other neutral oil

Combine the aquafaba, vinegar, mustard, syrup, and a generous pinch of salt in a blender (or in a large jar and use an immersion blender), and pulse until foamy, about 30 to 45 seconds.

In a very slow and steady stream, pour in the grapeseed oil until completely incorporated and the mixture is thick and emulsified. Season to taste with more salt. Store the aquafaba mayonnaise in an airtight container in the refrigerator for up to 1 week.

Falafel Mezze Bowls

For the falafel

2 cups dry chickpeas

1 teaspoon baking soda

1 cup fresh parsley

½ cup fresh cilantro

¼ cup fresh dill

1 medium yellow onion, roughly chopped

8 garlic cloves, peeled and crushed

Zest of 1 lemon

1 tablespoon ground cumin

1 tablespoon ground coriander

2 teaspoons smoked paprika

½ teaspoon cayenne

Sea salt and freshly ground black pepper

1½ teaspoons baking powder

2 tablespoons toasted sesame seeds

Grapeseed oil or other neutral oil, for frying

For the grain salad

¼ cup extra-virgin olive oil

2 tablespoons red wine vinegar

2 teaspoons dried oregano

Sea salt and freshly ground black pepper

3 cups cooked quinoa (couscous or wild rice work well too)

2 cups baby spinach

½ cup canned chickpeas, drained and rinsed

½ cup chopped dried apricots

I ate a lot of falafel during my years as a traveling musician, and I still love it, especially when you find a late-night spot that makes it with the works: a pita jam-packed with crisp, hot, freshly fried herby falafel; a smear of garlicky hummus; some pickled vegetables; and if you're especially lucky, maybe some roasted eggplant and french fries tucked in there, too. So. Damn. Good.

I let my memories of late-night street food guide me in preparing this recipe, an at-home bowl version of those handheld falafel sandwiches. I know this recipe looks long, but you can break it into components and make some of it—like the grain salad, hummus, and basil pesto—ahead, or even purchase good-quality store-bought hummus and pesto to make it easier. Note that the falafel are made with dried chickpeas, which need to be soaked overnight, but will maximize deliciousness.

Make the Falafel: In a large bowl, combine the chickpeas and baking soda. Pour in cold water to cover by 2 inches. Cover and refrigerate overnight (about 8 to 12 hours), and then drain and rinse.

In a food processor fitted with a blade attachment, combine the chickpeas, parsley, cilantro, dill, onion, garlic, lemon zest, cumin, coriander, paprika, and cayenne. Season well with salt and pepper, and pulse until a paste-like consistency forms, with a few clumps remaining for texture. Transfer to a medium bowl, cover with plastic wrap, and refrigerate for 1 hour.

Stir the baking powder and sesame seeds into the falafel mixture. Form the mixture into small, 1½-inch-thick patties.

Line a rimmed baking sheet with paper towel. In a large Dutch oven or high-sided, heavy-bottomed pot, pour the grapeseed oil to a depth of 3 inches. Heat over medium heat until the oil reaches 375°F on a deep-frying thermometer. Working in batches, as necessary, drop the falafels in the hot oil and fry, turning as needed, until golden, crispy, and cooked through, about 3 to 5 minutes. Transfer to the prepared baking sheet to drain any excess oil. Let the oil return to 375°F between each batch.

Make the Grain Salad: In a medium bowl, mix together the olive oil, red wine vinegar, oregano, and a pinch of salt and pepper. Add the cooked grains, spinach, chickpeas, and apricots, and mix well. Taste and season with salt and pepper.

ingredients and recipe continue

For the cucumber-tomato salad

1 cup pitted kalamata olives

½ English cucumber, diced

2 cups cherry tomatoes, halved

2 tablespoons minced fresh basil

2 tablespoons extra-virgin olive oil

1 tablespoon freshly squeezed lemon juice

Sea salt and freshly ground black pepper

For assembly

1 batch hummus (page 223)

1 batch basil pesto (page 124)

½ cup crumbled feta cheese

2 cups baby arugula

Fresh basil, for garnish

2 to 3 large pita bread, torn, for serving

1 lemon, cut into wedges, for serving

Make the Cucumber-Tomato Salad: In a medium bowl, combine the olives, cucumber, cherry tomatoes, and basil. Drizzle with the olive oil and lemon juice, and season to taste with salt and pepper.

Build Your Mezze Bowls: In a low bowl, place a scoop of grain salad, several spoonfuls of the cucumber-tomato salad, a few falafels, a generous spoonful of hummus, a dollop of pesto, some crumbled feta, a few arugula leaves, and some basil. Serve with pita and lemon wedges alongside.

Grilled Corn and Market Vegetable Chowder

5 ears of sweet corn, husks removed

Extra-virgin olive oil, for drizzling

Sea salt and freshly ground black pepper

2 tablespoons unsalted butter

1 garlic clove, minced

1 medium onion, diced

1 small leek, white and light green parts only, finely chopped

1 large carrot, peeled and diced

2 celery stalks, diced

1 medium green zucchini, diced

1 pound Yukon Gold potatoes (about 3), peeled and diced

5 cups vegetable stock

2½ cups heavy (35%) cream

¼ cup sliced green onions

¼ cup flat-leaf parsely

1 to 2 red chilies, thinly sliced (optional)

When the Maritime leaves turn to a reddish hue, but the farmer's market is still full to the brim with autumnal joys, I start to crave a big bowl of soul-warming chowder. For me, those hearty, veggie-packed soups, paired with a big hunk of crusty bread for dipping, are one of my favorite seasonal dishes. Bacon is often added to chowder, but in this robust plant-based rendition, the corn is grilled to add a layer of smoky complexity instead. In addition to the traditional hearty potatoes, I add zucchini to my chowder, but you could most definitely substitute or add other vegetables depending on what is available and in season at your local farmer's market.

Preheat a grill for direct, high-heat grilling (see Notes on Grilling, page 187).

Drizzle the corn with a bit of the olive oil, rubbing to coat on all sides, and then season all over with salt and pepper. Place the corn on the grill and cook, covered, turning occasionally, until lightly charred on all sides, about 10 minutes. Remove the corn from the grill and, when cool enough to handle, cut the kernels from the ears and set aside. Discard the ears.

Melt the butter in a large Dutch oven or stockpot over medium heat. When the butter has melted, add the garlic and cook, stirring, for 30 seconds, taking care that it doesn't burn. Add the onion, leek, carrot, and celery, and season with a pinch of salt. Cook, stirring often, until the vegetables have softened, about 7 to 8 minutes. Stir in the zucchini and potatoes. Pour in the stock, cream, and corn kernels, and mix well. Season with a few pinches of salt and pepper.

Bring to a boil over medium-high heat, reduce the heat to medium-low, and simmer until the potatoes are fork-tender and the soup has thickened, about 15 to 20 minutes. Taste and adjust the seasoning as necessary.

Divide the chowder into bowls. Top with green onions, parsley, pepper, a drizzle of olive oil, and if you like it spicy, a few slices of fresh chili. Yum!

Market Tomato Soup with Mozzarella and Pesto

For the soup

2 pounds mixed market tomatoes (as many kinds as you can get your hands on)

1 large white onion, roughly chopped

1 tablespoon minced fresh rosemary

1 head garlic

2 tablespoons extra-virgin olive oil

Sea salt and freshly ground black pepper

1 cup hot vegetable stock

1 tablespoon pure maple syrup

6 sundried tomatoes in oil

1 tablespoon red wine vinegar

1 tablespoon lemon zest

½ cup fresh basil, plus more for garnish

For the pesto

⅓ cup roasted pine nuts

½ cup freshly grated Parmesan cheese

2 garlic cloves, minced

1 tablespoon lemon zest

2 cups packed fresh basil

Sea salt and freshly ground black pepper

½ cup extra-virgin olive oil

For serving

2 balls (each 4 ounces) buffalo milk mozzarella, torn into pieces

Your favorite crusty bread

Tomato soup with a buttery grilled cheese sandwich alongside is a heavenly combination that always takes me right back to childhood. It's simple, and it's perfect. But tomato soup made from scratch with fresh tomatoes beats anything from a can and is well worth the effort. The tomatoes are roasted to concentrate their natural sugars and sundried tomatoes—those mainstays of the nineties—deepen the flavor. Instead of serving a sandwich alongside, I top each serving with some fresh buffalo milk mozzarella and a generous spoonful of homemade pesto. If you're short on time, you can use store-bought. And, of course, feel free to add a crispy golden grilled cheese sandwich alongside (like I often do).

Preheat the oven (or grill) to 400°F, and line a large rimmed baking sheet with parchment paper.

Make the Soup: Quarter the larger tomatoes and halve the small tomatoes, and then spread them out onto the prepared baking sheet. Add the onions and rosemary. Cut about ¼ inch off the top of the garlic head, exposing the cloves but leaving the root intact. Place the garlic on the baking sheet. Drizzle the olive oil over everything, season with salt and pepper, and mix well to coat. Roast for about 45 minutes, until the tomatoes are softened and nicely caramelized.

Squeeze the soft garlic cloves out of the garlic skins; discard the skins. In a blender or food processor, combine the roasted vegetables, stock, syrup, sundried tomatoes, vinegar, lemon zest, roasted garlic, and basil. Blend until smooth. Taste and adjust the seasoning as necessary. Transfer the soup to a large saucepan set over medium-low heat. Let the soup bubble away, stirring often, for 5 minutes.

Make the Pesto: Combine the pine nuts, Parmesan, garlic, lemon zest, and basil in the base of a food processor. Season with a pinch of salt and pepper then pulse while slowly streaming in the olive oil until completely incorporated. Taste and adjust the seasoning as necessary.

Spoon your soup into bowls. Top each with a generous portion of the mozzarella and drizzle on some of the pesto. Serve hot, with crusty bread alongside.

Mushroom Ragù with Cheesy Grits

For the grits

1 cup stone-ground grits

Sea salt

1 cup whole milk

⅔ cup grated aged cheddar cheese

⅔ cup grated Gruyère cheese

¼ cup grated Parmesan cheese

1 tablespoon unsalted butter

Freshly ground black pepper

For the ragù

2 tablespoons extra-virgin olive oil

2 tablespoons unsalted butter

4 garlic cloves, minced

½ teaspoon red pepper flakes

2 leeks, white and light green parts only, diced

Sea salt

2 pounds mixed mushrooms (the more variety the better)

2 teaspoons chopped fresh thyme

2 teaspoons chopped fresh oregano

1 tablespoon tomato paste

¼ cup dry white wine

2 medium tomatoes, cored and diced

1½ cups Porcini Mushroom Stock (page 109)

½ cup heavy (35%) cream

1 tablespoon lemon zest

Freshly ground black pepper

2 tablespoons chopped fresh flat-leaf parsley

2 tablespoons finely chopped fresh chives

Mushrooms are simply amazing. Complex, umami-packed, microbiome friendly, delicious in about a million and one applications, and when cooked properly, a total textural delight. Even basic supermarkets now carry a wide array of mushrooms, from button and brown to oyster, shiitake, and beyond. The world is your oyster (mushroom).

This recipe is inspired by another of my Chef's Manifesto compatriots, Chef Arthur Potts Dawson from London, England. Arthur is a champion of sustainability and creating a waste-free, planet-friendly kitchen, a personal mentor of mine, and a lover of all things mushrooms. Ever-preaching the mushroom gospel, this recipe is based on a dish that he created for one of our SDG2 Action Hubs at his beautiful space, OmVed Gardens in Highgate, London. For this ragù, I like to use as many different mushroom varieties as I can, which gives it the best texture and beautiful depth of flavor.

Prepare the Grits: In a large saucepan, bring 3 cups of water to a boil over medium-high heat. Stir in the grits, season with salt, and then reduce the temperature to medium-low. Let the grits gently cook and bubble away, stirring frequently, for 30 minutes. Stir in the milk and cook 10 minutes more, still stirring, until the grits are super-creamy. Gradually stir in the cheeses, a handful at a time, until melted and smooth. Stir in the butter, and season with salt and pepper. Cover to keep warm (see Cooking Note).

Make the Ragù: Heat the olive oil and butter in a large skillet over medium heat. When the butter has melted, add the garlic and red pepper flakes and cook for 30 seconds, keeping a close watch so that the garlic doesn't burn. Add the leeks, season with a pinch of salt, and cook until softened, about 4 to 5 minutes. Add the mushrooms, thyme, and oregano, season again with a pinch of salt, and cook, stirring often, until the mushrooms have released most of their liquid, about 10 minutes.

Stir in the tomato paste and white wine, and bring to a boil. Cook for about 5 minutes, until the wine has almost entirely evaporated. Stir in the tomatoes, and then the porcini stock, cream, and lemon zest. Bring back to a boil, and then reduce the heat to medium-low and cook until the ragù is thickened and beautiful, about 15 minutes. Season to taste with salt and pepper, and stir in the parsley.

Divide the grits into bowls and spoon over the mushroom ragù. Garnish with chives and serve.

Cooking Note: *I spent a few years living in Nashville, and one of the things I learned there is that for grits with the creamiest, most wonderful texture, you must cook them for the full 40 minutes. Also, life hack—if you want to make the grits in advance and keep them warm, transfer them to a heatproof bowl, cover it, and set it over a saucepan of simmering water until ready to serve.*

Rustic Ratatouille with Goat Cheese and Garlicky Baguette

For the ratatouille

¼ cup extra-virgin olive oil, divided

2 eggplants, diced

3 red bell peppers, stemmed, seeded, and diced

2 yellow summer squash, diced

2 medium green zucchini, diced

Sea salt

2 red onions, chopped

4 garlic cloves, minced

2 teaspoons chopped fresh thyme

¼ teaspoon red pepper flakes

1 teaspoon smoked paprika

4 large vine-ripened tomatoes, cored and chopped

2 cups passata (tomato purée)

1½ tablespoons balsamic vinegar

Juice of ½ lemon

1 tablespoon lemon zest

Freshly grated black pepper

½ cup fresh basil, plus more for garnish

For the baguette

1 baguette, thinly sliced on the bias

½ cup extra-virgin olive oil

¼ cup finely grated Parmesan cheese

6 garlic cloves, minced

2 teaspoons minced fresh thyme

2 teaspoons minced fresh rosemary

Sea salt and freshly ground black pepper

For serving

7 ounces crumbled fresh goat cheese (chèvre)

Extra-virgin olive oil

Freshly ground black pepper

Ratatouille certainly runs the gamut from haute cuisine to French country-style, all variations having a very important place in the culinary landscape. And as beautiful as our mouse friend Remy's version was, my heart will always lean toward rustic, family-style cooking. When the summer vegetables start coming in fast, this is the thing to make, as it helps you deal with the bounty in the most delicious way possible. You can use more or less of any of the vegetables specified here, so long as you keep the total amount about the same. And while this recipe needs no embellishment, if you're feeling extra motivated, a spoonful of salsa verde (page 84) or basil pesto (page 124) over each serving is beyond delicious.

Make the Ratatouille: Heat 2 tablespoons of the olive oil in a large Dutch oven or high-sided pot over medium heat until the oil is shimmering. Carefully add the eggplant, peppers, squash, and zucchini, season with a pinch of salt, and cook, stirring until starting to brown all over, about 5 to 6 minutes. With a slotted spoon, transfer to a rimmed plate or baking sheet.

To the now empty pot, add the remaining 2 tablespoons of the olive oil, the onion, garlic, thyme, and red pepper flakes. Season with a pinch of salt, and cook until the onion is softened and translucent, about 8 to 10 minutes.

Return the browned vegetables to the pot. Stir in the paprika, tomatoes, passata, vinegar, lemon juice, and lemon zest. Cover, reduce the heat to medium-low, and cook, stirring occasionally, for 30 to 35 minutes, until reduced and stew-y. Taste and season with salt and pepper.

Prepare the Baguette: Preheat the oven to 450°F and line a large baking sheet with parchment paper. Arrange the baguette slices on the baking sheet in a single layer. In a medium bowl, combine the olive oil, Parmesan, garlic, thyme, rosemary, and a nice pinch of salt and pepper, and mix well. Brush your baguette slices generously with the garlicky goodness, and then bake until golden brown, about 5 to 7 minutes.

Stir ½ cup of the basil into the ratatouille. Divide among bowls. Top with the goat cheese, a drizzle of olive oil, extra basil leaves, and a crack of black pepper. Serve warm, with the warm garlicky baguette slices alongside.

Spicy Chipotle Sweet Potato Bake with Black Beans and Feta

8 sweet potatoes
(about 2½ pounds)

¼ cup extra-virgin olive oil, divided

4 chipotles in adobo sauce, minced, divided

Sea salt

2 medium red onions, sliced

6 garlic cloves, minced

2 cups passata (tomato purée)

1 cup vegetable stock

1 can (15 ounces) black beans, drained and rinsed

1 can (15 ounces) chickpeas, drained and rinsed

1 teaspoon cinnamon

1 teaspoon smoked paprika

1 teaspoon ground cumin

½ teaspoon crushed red pepper flakes

Zest of 1 lime

Freshly ground black pepper

7 ounces crumbled feta

⅓ cup minced fresh cilantro, for garnish

Lime wedges, for serving

God bless the king of weeknight meals: the tray bake. Without a doubt, it has to be the greatest thing to happen to home cooks since the slow cooker. My favorite bit? It allows you to make a full meal with a minimum number of dishes, which is more than appealing. This recipe is, if we're being technical, a two-tray pan bake—one baking sheet for the roasted spuds, and a high-sided pan for a boldly spiced bean mixture that gets spooned over the potatoes once they're tender. A sprinkling of salty feta cheese and fresh cilantro on top completes this comforting vegetable-packed meal.

Preheat the oven to 400°F. Line a baking sheet with parchment paper.

With a sharp knife, cut a cross on top of each sweet potato, and then arrange the potatoes on the prepared baking sheet.

In a small bowl, combine 2 tablespoons of the olive oil with 2 teaspoons of the minced chipotle, and season with salt. Mix to combine, and brush over each sweet potato. Bake until you can easily pierce the potatoes with a knife, about 1 hour.

In a 9 x 13-inch baking dish, combine the onions, garlic, and the remaining 2 tablespoons of the oil, and season with salt. Stir to coat and roast for 10 minutes, or until the onion is softened and translucent. Pour the passata and stock into the baking dish, add the remaining chipotle, black beans, chickpeas, cinnamon, paprika, cumin, red pepper flakes, and lime zest. Season with salt and pepper, and mix well. Transfer to the oven to cook alongside the sweet potatoes until the sauce is thickened, reduced, and bubbling, about 30 to 35 minutes.

Transfer the cooked sweet potatoes to a serving platter, spoon the beans and sauce over and around the potatoes, and top with feta and cilantro. Serve with lime wedges and a cold beer, for good measure.

Fully Loaded Enchiladas

For the sauce

2 tablespoons extra-virgin olive oil

2 tablespoons all-purpose flour

¼ cup chili powder

½ teaspoon garlic powder

½ teaspoon ground cumin

¼ teaspoon dried oregano

2 cups vegetable stock

Sea salt

For the enchiladas

3 cups peeled and cubed butternut squash

¼ cup extra-virgin olive oil, divided

Sea salt and freshly ground black pepper

1 medium red onion, diced

1 red bell pepper, diced

2 tablespoons tomato paste

2 garlic cloves, minced

1 cup cooked basmati rice

1 can (15 ounces) black beans, drained and rinsed

1 teaspoon chili powder

½ teaspoon ground cumin

Zest of 1 lime

¼ cup chopped fresh cilantro, plus more for garnish

10 to 12 flour tortillas (8 inches)

1 cup grated sharp cheddar cheese

1 cup grated Monterey Jack cheese

For serving

¼ cup sour cream

1 avocado, sliced

¼ cup thinly sliced green onions

Hot sauce, homemade (page 216) or store-bought

Lime wedges

Enchiladas are perfect little cheesy, sauce-soaked packages of goodness, and built for cold-weather family-style meals. While you can certainly vary the filling depending on what you have on hand—this combination of roasted squash, rice, and beans is hearty and perfect for fall. Top that with a beautiful spice-packed sauce, a heaping helping of cheese, and all the fixings, and this recipe is sure to be a hit. Though you can purchase prepared enchilada sauce, I prefer to make my own. It comes together quickly and, if you use fresh spices (that is, dried spices that are no more than six months old), it will have a bright flavor that's unmatched by anything from a jar or can.

Make the Sauce: Heat the olive oil in a medium saucepan over medium heat. When the oil is warm, whisk in the flour and cook, whisking, until toasted, about 2 minutes. Whisk in the chili and garlic powders, the cumin and oregano, and the stock, and bring to a simmer. Let the sauce bubble away for about 5 minutes, or until starting to thicken and become glossy. Season to taste with salt, and set aside.

Preheat the oven to 400°F. Line a baking sheet with parchment paper.

Make the Enchiladas: Arrange the butternut squash on the baking sheet, drizzle with 2 tablespoons of the olive oil, and season with salt and pepper. Roast for 30 to 35 minutes, stirring halfway through, until fork-tender and starting to brown. Do not turn the oven off.

Heat the remaining 2 tablespoons of the olive oil in a large skillet over medium heat. Carefully add the onion, season with a pinch of salt, and cook until softened and translucent, about 6 to 8 minutes. Add the bell pepper, tomato paste, and garlic and cook for 2 minutes. Stir in the rice, black beans, chili powder, cumin, lime zest, and cilantro, and season with salt to taste. Fold in the butternut squash.

Pour ½ cup of the enchilada sauce into a 9 x 13-inch baking dish. Spoon about ½ cup of the squash mixture into the center of a tortilla, roll, and place, seam side down, in the baking dish. Repeat with the remaining tortillas. Spoon the enchilada sauce over and top with the cheddar and Jack cheeses. Bake for 20 to 25 minutes, or until the cheese has melted and is beginning to brown. Let rest for 5 minutes, and then serve with sour cream, avocado, green onions, hot sauce, cilantro, and lime wedges. Yes, please!

Under the Sea

I grew up in Riverview, a stone's throw from Moncton, and after traveling all over the world and living in a handful of other places, I returned here for good. Moncton is the largest city in the small but mighty Maritime province of New Brunswick, located on the eastern coast of Canada, bordering Maine. The city is at the end of the narrow Petitcodiac estuary, which flows into the Bay of Fundy. With relatively little coastal build-up and boat traffic and the warmest waters north of Virginia, New Brunswick is a pretty spectacular place to live. Within a short drive of the city, there are oyster farms (the province produces around 24 *million* oysters each year) and fishing villages where you can purchase freshly caught seafood straight off the boat. From the fishermen to the boat builders, processing plants, and fish markets, our little province really is the lobster (and arguably the cold-water shellfish) capital of the world.

Living here has undoubtedly influenced my undying passion for seafood. I grew up eating lobster on the regular, not realizing until I was much older that most people consider it a special occasion food. I learned how to shuck an oyster when I was just a kid. If my early experiences with seafood were centered on lobster rolls and oysters on the half shell, my travels have given me the opportunity to try seafood around the globe, from Mediterranean sea bass in Malta to lionfish in St. Lucia.

I can't talk about seafood, however, without talking about sustainability. With overfishing and climate change devastating the seafood industry, it's vitally important that we, as consumers and cooks, purchase and eat only sustainable seafood. Choosing sustainable seafood, which is seafood that is caught or farmed in ways that consider the long-term vitality of harvested species and the well-being of the oceans, as well as the livelihoods of fisheries-dependent communities, ensures that we'll be able to enjoy the bounty of the sea for generations to come. Both wild-caught and farmed fish and shellfish are managed under a system of enforced environmentally responsible practices that prevent overfishing, rebuild depleted stocks, minimize bycatch of protected species, and conserve essential fish habitats. You should not be shy about asking at the grocery store or fish market if the seafood you're thinking about buying is sustainable. And if it's not, you should consider other options.

In this chapter I'm sharing some of my favorite seafood recipes—dishes I grew up eating, like fish cakes and chowder, and the recipes I discovered elsewhere, like peel-and-eat shrimp with a fiery Caribbean-style hot sauce, branzino with tomato-caper sauce, and ponzu tuna. I hope you'll give them a try and that, someday, you might make your way up to Moncton to see its beauty for yourself. You might find me on Aboiteau Beach on the Acadian Shores, digging a pit in the sand for a clambake. I'll save you a beer.

Grilled Peel-and-Eat Shrimp with Caribbean-Style Hot Pepper Sauce

For the sauce

5 habanero peppers, stemmed, seeded, and chopped

1 mango, peeled, pitted, and diced

1 small yellow onion, diced

4 garlic cloves, minced

1 tablespoon minced fresh ginger

½ cup white vinegar

¼ cup pineapple juice

2 tablespoons pure maple syrup

½ teaspoon ground allspice

¼ teaspoon ground cumin

1 teaspoon sea salt

For the shrimp

2 pounds large (U26 to 30) shell-on shrimp

3 tablespoons extra-virgin olive oil

1 tablespoon smoked paprika

1½ teaspoons sweet paprika

½ teaspoon ground cumin

¼ teaspoon cayenne pepper

4 garlic cloves, very finely minced

Zest of 1 lime

½ teaspoon fine sea salt

Flaky salt, for serving

Lime wedges, for serving

This dish is inspired by my friend Alvin Franklin, the King of Hot Sauce, who I had the great privilege to cook alongside in gorgeous St. Croix. Alvin's Hot Pepper Sauce is an almost staple ingredient in both home kitchens and on restaurant tables in that part of the Caribbean. When I tried it, I immediately got the hiccups and a ruby red blush on my face that lasted for hours. This is my version of his spicy-sweet, fruity hot sauce. Be warned! This hot pepper sauce is very, extremely, unbelievably over-the-top spicy. Not for the faint of heart, but once you start eating it, it's hard to stop.

While the hot sauce might be the star of this recipe, the simple peel-and-eat shrimp, grilled in their shells so they retain moisture, are fun to make for a crowd. Set out a big platter of the shrimp with the hot sauce alongside, and encourage everyone to get their hands dirty peeling and dipping.

Make the Sauce: Place the habanero peppers, mango, onion, garlic, ginger, vinegar, pineapple juice, syrup, allspice, cumin, and salt in a high-powered blender, and blend until silky smooth. Transfer to a large saucepan, and bring to a boil over medium-high heat. Reduce the heat and simmer for about 10 minutes, until thickened. Cool to room temperature before transferring to an airtight container. Note that this recipe makes more sauce than you'll eat in a sitting, but any leftover sauce will keep in a jar in the refrigerator for months and is great on everything from eggs to tacos.

Preheat a grill for direct, high-heat grilling (see Notes on Grilling, page 187).

Prepare the Shrimp: In a large bowl, combine the shrimp, olive oil, smoked and sweet paprika, cumin, cayenne, garlic, and lime zest. Season with the salt, and toss to mix well. Transfer the shrimp to the preheated grill, arranging them in a single layer, and cook for 2½ minutes. Flip and continue cooking on the second side for 2½ minutes more, or until the shells are crispy and the shrimp are pink, opaque, and cooked through.

Transfer to a platter, and sprinkle with flaky salt. Serve with the lime wedges and hot sauce alongside (and maybe a cold beer).

Cooking Note: *Word to the wise: Wear plastic gloves when chopping the habanero chilies. Not only can the compounds in the peppers irritate your skin, but the residual oils can also wreak havoc should you rub your eyes or lick your fingers, even hours later.*

Shrimp

Though there are 3000 species of shrimp, only four wild-caught shrimp are considered sustainable: pink shrimp from Oregon, spot prawns from the Pacific Northwest, pink and brown Gulf shrimp, and any shrimp from US and Canadian waters in the northern Atlantic. If you can't find wild-caught shrimp, farmed shrimp can be a good option, with some caveats—look for shrimp farmed in the United States, which are generally considered eco-friendly, and read the label or ask at the store if the shrimp you're buying have been treated with preservatives. Don't be afraid to purchase frozen (or previously frozen) shrimp; the vast majority of shrimp are frozen, and if they are thawed carefully they will taste every bit as good as hard-to-find never-frozen shrimp. If you plan ahead, the easiest way to properly thaw shrimp is to place them in the refrigerator overnight, or about 12 hours, so they can gently defrost. Once defrosted, be sure to use them within 48 hours. If you're short on time, submerge the unopened bag of frozen shrimp in a big bowl of cold water, weighing it down with a plate so it stays submerged, and let stand for about 45 minutes.

Ponzu Tuna with Crispy Wontons and Papaya Salsa

I've had the good fortune to spend time in Hawaii, otherwise known as paradise on earth. Hawaiian food is heavily influenced by Japanese, Chinese, Filipino, Tahitian, and Portuguese cuisines, which reflect the island's history of settlement and immigration. The lush tropical climate and pristine waters also give Hawaiian cooks a big advantage— you don't need to do much to a piece of beautiful ahi tuna to make it delicious.

The marinade I use for the fish includes a few Japanese ingredients, including mirin, kombu (a type of edible kelp), and bonito. Bonito, also known as katsuobushi, is a staple ingredient in Japanese cuisine, and for good reason—it adds incredible depth and umami. Finished pieces of katsuobushi are as hard as wood, and before they are used they're shaved on a razor-sharp grater into papery ribbons, which is how it's typically sold (pre-shaved). You can purchase bonito, kombu, and mirin at Asian grocery stores and online, or in some supermarkets, where it's often stocked near the seaweed.

For the ponzu sauce

½ cup soy sauce

Zest of 1 lemon

¼ cup freshly squeezed lemon juice

2 tablespoons freshly squeezed orange juice

2 tablespoons freshly squeezed lime juice

2 tablespoons mirin

½ cup dried bonito flakes

1 piece kombu

For the rice

2 cups jasmine rice

3 tablespoons rice vinegar

Zest of 1 lime

2 tablespoons sugar

2 teaspoons kosher salt

For the salsa

1 large papaya, peeled, seeded, and diced

1 mango, peeled and diced

½ medium red onion, diced

1 jalapeño pepper, stemmed and minced (for a less spicy salsa, seed the chili before mincing)

¼ cup minced fresh cilantro

Pinch of sugar

Juice of 2 limes

Sea salt

Make the Ponzu Sauce: Combine the soy sauce, lemon zest, lemon juice, orange juice, lime juice, mirin, bonito flakes, and kombu in a large jar with a lid. Seal the jar and give it a quick shake to mix. Transfer to the fridge and refrigerate overnight (or about 12 hours). Strain through a fine-mesh strainer into a clean jar and discard the bonito and kombu. Store the ponzu sauce in an airtight container in the refrigerator for up to 1 week.

Prepare the Rice: Rinse the rice several times in cold running water until the water runs clear (this helps wash off the excess starch, which can make the rice sticky). In a medium saucepan, combine 4 cups of water, the rice vinegar, lime zest, sugar, and salt and bring to a boil over high heat. Stir in the rice, cover with a lid, reduce the heat to low, and cook for 15 minutes. Remove the pot from the heat, let stand, covered, for 10 minutes, and then fluff with a fork. Set aside.

Make the Salsa: In a medium bowl, combine the papaya, mango, onion, jalapeño, cilantro, sugar, and lime juice. Mix well, and season to taste with salt. Refrigerate until ready to serve, up to 1 hour.

Make the Wontons: In a large Dutch oven or high-sided, heavy-bottomed pot, pour the avocado oil to a depth of 1½ inches. Heat over medium heat until the oil reaches 350°F on a deep-frying thermometer. Line a baking sheet with paper towel and set nearby. Working in batches, carefully drop a small handful of wonton wrappers in the hot oil, and fry until golden brown and crispy all over, 2 to 3 minutes. Transfer to the prepared baking sheet and season with salt. Repeat with the remaining wonton wrappers, letting the oil return to 350°F between each batch.

ingredients and recipe continue

For the wontons

Avocado oil or other neutral oil, for deep-frying

25 wonton wrappers

Sea salt

For the tuna

1 boneless ahi tuna fillet (1½ to 2 pounds), skin removed

Sea salt and freshly ground black pepper

1 tablespoon avocado oil or other neutral oil

For serving

2 teaspoons toasted sesame seeds

¼ cup fresh cilantro

2 avocados, pitted, peeled, and sliced

Prepare the Tuna: Season both sides of the tuna with salt and pepper. Heat the avocado oil in a large nonstick skillet over medium-high heat until the oil is shimmering. Carefully place the tuna in the skillet and sear for 1 minute each on all four sides, keeping a very close watch to ensure it sears evenly. Transfer to a plate. Pour the ponzu sauce into the hot skillet and bring to a simmer. Place the tuna back in the skillet and cook for 1 more minute on each side (or longer if you like your tuna less rare). Return the tuna to the plate and pour any sauce remaining in the skillet over the fish. Let rest for a few minutes, and then thinly slice the tuna.

To serve, transfer the tuna to a serving dish and sprinkle the sesame seeds and cilantro over. Serve with the rice, salsa, fried wontons, and sliced avocado alongside.

Cooking Note: *You'll want to use a ripe papaya for the salsa. When its skin has turned from green to yellow and it's soft to the touch, it's good to go.*

Gingery Tuna Tartare with Crispy Potato Matchsticks

For the potato matchsticks

4 large unpeeled russet potatoes

Grapeseed oil or other neutral oil, for frying

1½ tablespoons furikake

Sea salt

Sriracha, for serving

For the tartare

1 pound sushi-grade bluefin tuna

1 teaspoon grated fresh ginger

1 tablespoon soy sauce

1 tablespoon freshly squeezed lime juice

1 jalapeño pepper, stemmed, seeded, and minced

2 teaspoons toasted sesame oil

1 teaspoon extra-virgin olive oil

1½ tablespoons minced fresh chives

1 tablespoon toasted sesame seeds

4 large egg yolks

Tuna tartare is something most people consider restaurant food, as opposed to something you might make at home, but it's really a breeze to prepare, provided you can source sushi-grade fish. Be sure to chat with your local fishmonger for help sourcing the best-quality tuna. They're the experts! Because this is a raw preparation, make sure that your fish is absolutely fresh and pristine; it's not inexpensive, but is a worthy splurge.

The matchsticks (allumettes in French) are the salty, crispy shoestring fries of your dreams. Take care to slice the potatoes thinly and evenly, fry them in batches so they brown quickly, and try not to eat them all before you serve the tartare! And if you need a shortcut, or it's much too hot outside to heat oil for deep-frying, this tartare is equally good served with salty potato chips.

Prepare the Potato Matchsticks: Using a mandoline fitted with a julienne blade (or a very sharp and steady knife), cut the potatoes into matchsticks. Transfer to a bowl of ice water and soak for 20 minutes.

Make the Tartare: While the spuds soak, slice the tuna into thin planks. Stack a few of the planks and thinly cut them lengthwise into ¼-inch-thick batons. Cut the batons crosswise into ¼-inch cubes. Repeat until you've diced all the tuna. Transfer to a bowl and add the ginger, soy sauce, lime juice, jalapeño, sesame oil, olive oil, chives, and toasted sesame seeds, and mix well. Cover and refrigerate while you finish the potatoes.

Finish the Potato Matchsticks: Drain the potatoes and dry completely with paper towel.

In a large Dutch oven or high-sided, heavy-bottomed pot, pour the oil to a depth of 3 inches. Heat over medium heat until the oil reaches 350°F on a deep-frying thermometer. Line a rimmed baking sheet with paper towel and set nearby. Working in small batches, fry the potatoes until golden and crispy, about 2½ to 3 minutes per batch. Transfer to the prepared baking sheet and repeat with the remaining potatoes. When all of the potatoes have been fried, transfer to a bowl and toss with furikake and a few generous pinches of salt.

Divide the tartare between four plates. Top each serving with an egg yolk. Serve with a generous pile of potato matchsticks and sriracha for dipping. To eat, stir the egg yolk into the tuna.

Grilled Sardines with Gremolata

For the sardines

¼ cup extra-virgin olive oil

2 tablespoons fresh rosemary leaves

1 tablespoon smoked paprika

Zest of 1 lemon

4 garlic cloves, minced

¼ teaspoon sea salt

¼ teaspoon freshly ground black pepper

8 large sardines, scaled, gutted, and heads removed

2 lemons, halved, for grilling

For the gremolata

2 heaping packed cups fresh flat-leaf parsley, finely chopped

Zest of 1 Meyer or Eureka lemon

1 tablespoon freshly squeezed Meyer or Eureka lemon juice

4 garlic cloves, minced

1 small jalapeño or serrano chili, stemmed, seeded, and minced

½ cup extra-virgin olive oil

Sea salt

In North America, most people are only familiar with canned sardines, which, while tasty, are only one way to enjoy these sustainable and delicious fishes. I love to grill sardines—they cook quickly, the hot fire crisping the skin to golden perfection without drying out the rich meat. Because sardines are an oily fish, I like to serve them with an assertive, acid-forward condiment like this gremolata, which helps cut through the richness. Perfect Mediterranean-inspired eating.

Prepare the Sardines: In a medium bowl, stir together the olive oil, rosemary, paprika, lemon zest, garlic, salt, and pepper. Pour into a high-sided baking dish (or large resealable storage bag), add the sardines, and toss to coat. Cover and marinate in the fridge for 4 hours.

Make the Gremolata: In a small bowl, combine the parsley, lemon zest, lemon juice, garlic, chili, and olive oil, and mix well. Season with salt to taste, and set aside.

Grill the Sardines: Preheat a grill for direct, high-heat grilling (see Notes on Grilling, page 187). Place the sardines directly on the grill grate, and grill for 4 to 5 minutes per side, until crispy on the outside, and the flesh is opaque and flakes easily with a fork. During the last half of the grilling time, add the halved lemons to the grill grate, cut side down, and grill until charred.

Transfer the sardines and grilled lemon halves to a serving platter, and sprinkle the gremolata over the fish. Serve hot or warm, squeezing the grilled lemons over the fish just before eating.

Crab Bisque with Rosemary Croutons

For the bisque

3 tablespoons unsalted butter

2 garlic cloves, minced

2 medium leeks, white and light green parts only, thinly sliced

2 celery stalks, finely chopped

1 red bell pepper, stemmed, seeded, and diced

Sea salt

1 teaspoon Old Bay seasoning

¼ teaspoon cayenne pepper

2 tablespoons tomato paste

3 tablespoons all-purpose flour

1 cup dry white wine

4 cups fish stock

Zest of 1 lemon

½ cup heavy (35%) cream

1½ pounds cooked snow crab meat

Freshly ground black pepper

¼ cup fresh basil leaves

For the croutons

½ large ciabatta loaf, torn into 1-inch pieces

¼ cup extra-virgin olive oil

3 tablespoons chopped fresh rosemary

3 garlic cloves, minced

¼ teaspoon smoked paprika

⅓ teaspoon cayenne pepper

Sea salt and freshly ground black pepper

Between lobster seasons in New Brunswick, the fishermen pivot to catching snow crabs, and cooks pivot, too. We gobble up the sweet, briny crab meat, piling it in salads, using it in crab cakes, and in my house, making this bisque—perfect for warming your bones on cold coastal days. Snow crab meat is available outside my Maritime province, of course, where it's often sold frozen. You can substitute a different variety of crab if that's what is available near you. But please don't use imitation crab, which is nothing like the real McCoy. Traditionally, a bisque is a creamy, puréed French soup made from crustaceans; the shells are used to make the stock and the meat is added to the finished soup. For my simplified version I use fish stock instead of shellfish stock, and I don't add rice, which is often used to thicken the soup. A small amount of cream added at the end, along with a generous amount of crab meat, make the soup particularly luxurious, though it's easy enough to make on a weeknight.

Preheat the oven to 400°F and line a rimmed baking sheet with parchment paper.

Make the Bisque: Heat the butter in a large stockpot over medium heat. When the butter has melted, add the garlic and cook, stirring, for about 30 seconds (keeping a close watch so that it doesn't burn), until fragrant. Add the leeks, celery, and red pepper, season with a pinch of salt, and cook, stirring occasionally, until softened and translucent, about 5 to 6 minutes. Stir in the Old Bay, cayenne, and tomato paste, and cook for about 2 minutes, stirring so the vegetables are coated. Add the flour and cook, stirring, for 1 minute longer.

Pour in the wine, bring to a simmer, and then reduce until almost evaporated. Add the stock and lemon zest, and season with a few generous pinches of salt. Bring to a simmer, reduce the heat to medium-low, and let the bisque bubble away for about 30 minutes.

Prepare the Croutons: While the soup is simmering, place the ciabatta pieces on the prepared baking sheet, and drizzle generously with the olive oil. Add the rosemary, garlic, paprika, cayenne, and a pinch each of salt and pepper. Toss to mix well, transfer to the oven, and bake for about 20 to 25 minutes, stirring halfway through, until crisp and golden.

Finish the Soup: Remove the pot from the heat. Using an immersion blender (or standard blender, working in batches), purée the soup until silky smooth. Pour in the cream and add about ½ pound of the crab meat. Return the pot to the heat. Bring to a gentle simmer and simmer for 5 minutes. Taste and adjust the seasoning as necessary.

Ladle the bisque into warmed serving bowls. Top each bowl with a generous portion of the remaining crab meat, a bit of pepper, basil, and a small handful of golden croutons.

Classic Maritime Fish Chowder

2 tablespoons unsalted butter

2 garlic cloves, minced

1 medium yellow onion, finely chopped

1 cup diced celery

1 bay leaf

1 teaspoon chopped fresh thyme

Sea salt

2 large Yukon Gold potatoes (about 8 to 10 ounces), peeled and diced

2 cups fish stock

1½ cups whole milk

1½ cups heavy (35%) cream

½ teaspoon smoked paprika

Zest of 1 lemon

Freshly ground black pepper

2 pounds boneless, skinless white fish (cod or haddock work great), cut into ½-inch pieces

1 tablespoon chopped fresh dill

1 tablespoon finely chopped fresh chives

1 lemon, cut into wedges, for serving

In my part of the world, chowder is a religion. Every cook in New Brunswick probably has their own version of chowder, and this is mine. The important thing to keep in mind is that a fish chowder is only as good as the fish you put in it, so you should use whatever super-fresh white fish is best where you live. I like cod and haddock, mild and flaky varieties that are abundant where I live, but you could make this with halibut or pollock, or add cooked lobster, crab meat, or shrimp to the base, or shucked clams or oysters. Once you've added the milk and cream to the chowder, don't let it come to a boil, which can cause it to separate—a gentle simmer is hot enough to cook the fish. Low and slow, y'all. Serve the chowder with crusty bread for sopping up the flavorful brothy deliciousness.

In a large stockpot, melt the butter over medium heat. Add the garlic and cook, stirring, for 30 seconds, keeping a close watch so it doesn't burn. Add the onion, celery, bay leaf, thyme, and a pinch of salt, and cook, stirring, until softened, about 8 to 10 minutes.

Add the potatoes and fish stock, and bring to a boil over medium-high heat. Reduce the heat to medium, and simmer until the potatoes are almost fork-tender, about 6 to 8 minutes.

Stir in the milk, heavy cream, paprika, and lemon zest, season with salt and pepper, and bring the chowder back to a gentle simmer, stirring often. Add the fish and simmer for about 5 minutes, until the fish is cooked through and flakes easily with a fork. Taste and adjust the seasoning as necessary.

Ladle into warmed bowls. Garnish with dill and chives, and serve right away, with lemon wedges alongside.

Salmon, Potato, and Dill Soup with Crème Fraîche

2 tablespoons unsalted butter

2 garlic cloves, minced

1 medium yellow onion, diced

2 celery stalks, diced

Sea salt

1 tablespoon tomato paste

2 pounds new potatoes, halved

4 cups fish stock

2 bay leaves

1 pound boneless, skinless salmon fillet, pin bones removed (see Cooking Note, page 170), cut into 2-inch cubes

2 cups baby spinach

½ cup crème fraîche, plus more for serving

1 small bunch fresh dill, finely chopped, plus a small handful of dill for garnish

Freshly ground black pepper

Lemon wedges, for serving

This beautiful bowl of goodness takes inspiration from time spent cooking in Sweden during midsummer, at the start of the local growing season. Salmon and new potatoes are gospel for Swedes, and this recipe highlights how those two simple ingredients, when treated properly, can taste so luxurious. It's hearty and soul-warming but not heavy. Make this when new potatoes become available at your local farmer's market, and enter a world of Scandinavian-inspired bliss.

In a large Dutch oven or stockpot, melt the butter over medium heat. When the butter has melted, add the garlic and cook, stirring, for 30 seconds, keeping a close watch so that it doesn't burn. Add the onion and celery, season with a pinch of salt, and cook, stirring occasionally, until the vegetables are softened and translucent, about 6 to 8 minutes. Stir in the tomato paste and cook for 1 minute longer. Add the potatoes and cook, stirring often, for 5 minutes.

Pour in the fish stock and add the bay leaves. Season with salt and bring to a simmer. Let the soup bubble and simmer away for 10 minutes, until the potatoes are just fork-tender. Add the salmon and spinach, and gently cook for 5 minutes, until the fish is cooked through and the spinach is wilted. Remove from the heat, and stir in the crème fraîche, dill, and a pinch of pepper. Taste and adjust the seasoning as necessary.

Divide the soup among bowls. Top each serving with a spoonful of crème fraîche, some of the reserved dill, a grind of pepper, and serve with lemon wedges.

Grilled Octopus with Romesco and Crispy Potatoes

For the octopus

2 tablespoons sea salt

1 cup dry white wine

1 head garlic

Handful of fresh rosemary sprigs

1 tablespoon black peppercorns

3 pounds fresh octopus tentacles

¼ cup extra-virgin olive oil

For the potatoes

2 pounds russet potatoes, peeled and cut into 1-inch chunks

¼ cup extra-virgin olive oil

Sea salt

1 tablespoon minced fresh rosemary

1 tablespoon minced fresh thyme

1 lemon, cut into wedges

Freshly ground black pepper

For the romesco

1 large roasted red bell pepper (from a jar)

2 garlic cloves, roughly chopped

½ cup roasted slivered almonds

¼ cup passata (tomato purée)

2 tablespoons chopped fresh flat-leaf parsley

2 tablespoons sherry vinegar

1 teaspoon smoked paprika

1 small bird's eye or Thai chili, stemmed and very finely chopped

½ cup extra-virgin olive oil

Juice of ½ lemon

Sea salt and freshly ground black pepper

Octopus may not be the most common ingredient in North American kitchens, but throughout Europe—from Sicily to Spain to Greece—the cephalopod, which is related to squid and cuttlefish, gets top billing. And it's no wonder—it has a mild flavor, firm texture, and high nutritional value, and can be sustainably farmed. (When shopping, look for octopus that bears the blue label of the Marine Stewardship Council.) Generally speaking, octopus is best when cooked hot and fast, or slow and low—anything in between and the octopus can become extremely chewy. My method employs both techniques. The tentacles are first slowly simmered until tender, and then grilled over a hot fire until crispy and irresistibly charred.

When creating this dish, I was inspired by Spain, where they eat lots of octopus. It's frequently served with romesco—a nutty, tangy sauce made from red peppers and nuts, flavored with smoky paprika and brightened with a splash of sherry vinegar. The addition of roasted potatoes makes this a complete dish, just add a salad alongside for a full meal. If you'd like, serve the octopus and potatoes with mojo verde (page 157) instead of—or in addition to—the romesco.

Prepare the Octopus: Fill a large stockpot three-quarters full with water, and pour in the salt and wine. Cut about ¼ inch off the top of the head of garlic, exposing the cloves but leaving the root intact, and add it to the pot, along with the rosemary and peppercorns. Bring to a boil over medium-high heat.

Meanwhile, place the octopus on a cutting board, and use a meat mallet to pound the octopus tentacles several times, moving down from the thickest to thinnest part of each tentacle (this helps tenderize the meat). Using tongs, dip each tentacle into the boiling water 3 times, for about 2 to 3 seconds each time, until the tip of the tentacle curls up, and then drop the tentacle into the water. Return the water to a rapid boil, reduce the heat to low, and simmer for 1 to 2 hours, until the octopus is tender—you should be able to pierce the thickest part of the tentacle easily with a sharp knife. Remove from the heat, leaving the octopus submerged in the poaching liquid, and let cool to room temperature.

When cool, remove the skin from each tentacle by rubbing it with paper towel. Be careful not to remove the suckers, just the surrounding purple skin. Dry completely. The drier they are, the more the char will develop on the tentacles without overcooking them.

About an hour before you want to eat, prepare your potatoes and romesco sauce. Preheat the oven to 400°F. Line a baking sheet with parchment paper.

recipe continues

Prepare the Potatoes: Place the potatoes in a large saucepan and add cold water to cover by about 2 inches. Add a generous amount of salt to the pot, and bring to a boil over high heat. Boil for 7 minutes and then drain. Return the potatoes to the saucepan, pour in the olive oil and season with salt. Gently shake the saucepan a few times to help rough up the edges of the potato cubes. Transfer to the prepared baking sheet, sprinkle over the rosemary and thyme, add the lemon wedges, and season the potatoes with a good bit of pepper. Roast for 40 to 45 minutes, flipping halfway through, until super-crispy and golden brown.

Make the Romesco: Combine the bell pepper, garlic, almonds, passata, parsley, vinegar, paprika, and chili in a food processor, and pulse until finely chopped. With the machine running, add the oil in a slow and steady stream until all the oil has been added and the sauce is emulsified. Transfer to a bowl, stir in the lemon juice, and season to taste with salt and pepper. Store the romesco in an airtight container in the refrigerator for up to 3 days. Let it come to room temperature before serving.

Grill the Octopus: Prepare a grill for direct, high-heat grilling (see Notes on Grilling, page 187). Toss the octopus with the olive oil, season with salt, transfer to the grill, and cook about 8 minutes per side, until nicely caramelized and charred in spots. To serve, pile the potatoes and octopus on a platter, and serve the romesco sauce alongside.

MOJO VERDE

Like the romesco, this is a versatile sauce that is great on many different things. I like it with seafood of all kinds, but it's also terrific spooned over roast or grilled pork or chicken, and could even be used in place of the herbed vinaigrette on the steak sandwich on page 249.

MAKES ABOUT ¾ CUP

2 cups fresh cilantro

6 garlic cloves

Zest of ½ lemon

½ teaspoon ground cumin

¼ teaspoon cayenne pepper

Sea salt

½ cup extra-virgin olive oil

2 teaspoons sherry vinegar

In the bowl of a food processor, add the cilantro, garlic, lemon zest, cumin, cayenne, and a good pinch of salt. Pulse the mixture, scraping down the sides as necessary, until a smooth paste forms. With the machine running, add the oil in a slow and steady stream until all the oil has been added and the sauce is emulsified. Add the vinegar and pulse one final time. Transfer to a bowl, and season to taste with salt. Store the mojo in an airtight container in the refrigerator for up to 3 days. Let it come to room temperature before serving.

Clams with Sweet Corn, Tomato, and Grilled Bread

For the clams

¼ cup extra-virgin olive oil

¼ teaspoon crushed red pepper flakes

1 leek, white and light green parts only, trimmed and cut lengthwise, then thinly sliced crosswise into half-moons

Sea salt

2 garlic cloves, minced

2 tablespoons minced fresh tarragon

1 tablespoon tomato paste

1 cup fresh corn kernels

2 cups cherry tomatoes, halved

1½ cups dry white wine

Freshly ground black pepper

2 pounds steamer clams

For the bread

1 loaf sourdough, thickly sliced

Extra-virgin olive oil

Sea salt

1 garlic clove

For serving

2 tablespoons minced fresh flat-leaf parsley

Lemon wedges

Clams are total seaside rock stars—they're inexpensive, taste great, and cook in a flash. Though you can eat them all year long, I especially like to serve them in the summer, when you're looking for a fast, shareable, casual meal. For this recipe, I especially like to use steamer clams, which are medium-sized, with thin shells and sweet meat, but if you can't find them, you could substitute another small or medium clam variety, such as littlenecks. (Avoid larger clams, which are wonderful for chowder but are too giant—and often too chewy—for this preparation.) If you have a grill with a burner on one side, you can make the clams at the same time you grill the bread. Otherwise, grill the bread while the clams cook on the stovetop, or, if you're doing this all indoors, use a griddle pan to toast the bread.

Preheat a grill for medium-high grilling (see Notes on Grilling, page 187). If you don't have access to a grill, then use a griddle pan.

Prepare the Clams: Heat the olive oil and red pepper flakes in a large Dutch oven or stockpot over medium heat until the oil is shimmering. Carefully add the leeks, season with a pinch of salt, and cook until softened, 3 to 4 minutes. Add the garlic, tarragon, and tomato paste, and cook for 2 minutes, stirring often to make sure the mixture doesn't stick. Add the corn and cherry tomatoes. Pour in the wine, add a few grinds of pepper, and bring to a simmer. Add the clams and cover and cook for about 8 to 10 minutes, stirring every few minutes, or until the clams open.

Grill the Bread: Drizzle both sides of each slice of sourdough with olive oil. Season with salt, and grill the bread, turning once, until golden and charred on both sides. Rub the garlic clove on one side of each slice of bread, and pile on a plate.

Transfer the clams and their juices to a serving bowl, discarding any that haven't opened. Sprinkle with the parsley. Serve right away, with the grilled bread and lemon wedges alongside.

The Ultimate Lobster Roll

½ cup finely chopped celery

½ cup mayonnaise, homemade (page 118) or store-bought

¼ cup thinly sliced fresh chives

1 tablespoon minced fresh tarragon

1 tablespoon freshly squeezed lemon juice

Sea salt and freshly ground black pepper

1½ pounds cooked lobster meat, chopped into bite-size pieces

1 teaspoon Tabasco (or more, if you like it spicy)

4 tablespoons unsalted butter, soft, divided

6 split-top hotdog-style brioche rolls

2 tablespoons dill, for garnish

Fleur de sel, for garnish

Potato chips, for serving

Lemon wedges, for serving

When most folks think lobster, they think of the almighty lobster roll. That classic, handheld, golden-toasted bun filled to the brim with the King of the Sea. It's the quintessential summertime dish in the Maritimes. Growing up in Greater Moncton, just a short drive from Shediac, New Brunswick, I've been intimately connected with lobster for my entire life. Shediac is the home of the International Lobster Festival, and the super-cold, super-salty, and pristine waters of the Bay of Fundy and Northumberland Strait produce the best lobster on the planet. For Maritimers, the story of lobster goes far beyond just the dinner table. It's our heritage. It runs through our blood. And like clockwork, when lobster season is in full swing, we gather as one big family at the communal table celebrating the bounty of the sea.

This recipe is my version of a classic, and one that I make every chance I get. Lush lobster meat tossed with homemade mayonnaise, celery, lemon, herbs, and served up in a toasted brioche bun. A guaranteed hit at the dinner table, at the picnic table, or with your feet in the sand gazing into the ocean.

In a large bowl, combine the celery, mayonnaise, chives, tarragon, lemon juice, and a pinch of salt and pepper. Mix well. Stir in the lobster meat and Tabasco. Taste and adjust the seasoning with additional salt, pepper, or lemon juice. Cover with plastic wrap, and chill in the refrigerator for at least 30 minutes or up to 4 hours.

Heat 2 tablespoons of the butter in a large skillet over medium heat. When the butter has melted, working in batches, add the buns, and toast, flipping once and adding the remaining 2 tablespoons of the butter to the skillet, until golden on both sides.

Stuff the buns with the chilled lobster salad. Garnish with fresh dill and a sprinkle of fleur de sel. Serve with potato chips and lemon wedges on the side.

Cooking Note: *If preparing lobster rolls for an outdoor East Coast style-feast (as I often do), and you've got the grill warmed, I highly recommend grilling your buns. That kiss of smoky, charred, grilled goodness adds a beautiful depth of flavour to these lobster rolls.*

Panko-Crusted Fish Burgers

4 boneless, skinless white fish fillets (6 ounces each), such as cod, haddock, or halibut

Sea salt and freshly ground black pepper

½ cup all-purpose flour

2 large eggs, lightly whisked

1½ cups panko breadcrumbs

1 tablespoon lemon zest

2 tablespoons finely minced fresh chives

1 tablespoon finely chopped fresh tarragon

Grapeseed oil or other neutral oil, for frying

For serving

Tartar Sauce (page 165) or Tarragon Aioli (page 167)

4 brioche hamburger buns, split and toasted

1 large tomato, thinly sliced

4 lettuce leaves

This recipe is a tribute to my dad, whose eternal love of the Filet-O-Fish will forever baffle and astound me, though I still love him all the same. I vividly remember Dad sneaking my brother and me out when we were kids to eat copious amounts of fast food, with my health-conscious vegetarian mom being none the wiser. (Sorry, Mom.) I liked it as a kid, but as I got older I came to realize that a proper homemade fish burger is vastly superior to anything you can get from a drive-through. Crispy on the outside, juicy and fresh on the inside. Topped with homemade tartar sauce and wrapped up in a buttery toasted bun, this is a burger I absolutely can get behind. Perfect for curing your fast food cravings, with no sneaking around required.

Season the fish fillets on all sides with salt and pepper. Put the flour in one bowl, and the beaten eggs in another. In a third bowl, combine the panko, lemon zest, chives, and tarragon. Working with one piece of fish at a time, dredge the fish in the flour, then in the egg wash, letting the excess drip off, and finally in the panko mixture, turning so the fish is completely coated. Set on a plate.

In a large Dutch oven or high-sided, heavy-bottomed pot, pour the grapeseed oil to a depth of 1½ inches. Heat over medium heat until the oil reaches 350°F on a deep-frying thermometer. Line a plate with paper towel and set nearby. Carefully add the fish and fry, turning once, for about 3 minutes per side. Using tongs or a spider, transfer the fish to the prepared plate to drain. Season with salt.

Spread a tablespoon of tartar sauce on the bottom half of each bun. Top with the fish, a tomato slice, and lettuce. Spread a second table-spoon of tartar sauce on the inside of the top half of each bun, then press together and sandwich to your heart's delight.

Healthy-ish Fish and Chips

For the tartar sauce

½ cup mayonnaise, homemade (page 118) or store-bought, or aioli (without the tarragon, page 167)

2 tablespoons minced fresh dill

2 tablespoons minced capers

2 tablespoons finely chopped dill pickles

2 tablespoons freshly squeezed lemon juice

1 tablespoon finely minced fresh chives

1 garlic clove, minced

Sea salt and freshly ground black pepper

For the fish and chips

2 pounds Yukon Gold potatoes, cut into ¼-inch-thick batons

7 tablespoons extra-virgin olive oil, divided

Sea salt

1 cup panko breadcrumbs

2 teaspoons finely chopped fresh tarragon

1 garlic clove, minced

1 tablespoon lemon zest

¼ cup grated Parmesan cheese

Freshly ground black pepper

½ cup all-purpose flour

2 large eggs

1 tablespoon Dijon mustard

1½ pounds cod, haddock, or other white fish (about ¾ inch thick), cut into 4 even pieces

Victoria Day marks the unofficial season opener for fish and chips in Atlantic Canada. That's when the New Brunswick seaside restaurants that serve fried seafood open for the summer. On a warm evening, there's nothing better than dropping by for a basket of fried fish (or clams) and a pile of salty fries. Nothing, that is, other than the ability to make a healthful version anytime you want. In my version here, I bread the fish in a seasoned breadcrumb mixture that gives it a crunchy, flavorful coating—no deep-frying required. Homemade tartar sauce alongside (and a crisp beer or two) is an absolute must.

Make the Tartar Sauce: In a medium bowl, combine the mayonnaise, dill, capers, pickles, lemon juice, chives, and garlic, and season to taste with salt and pepper. Cover with plastic wrap and refrigerate until ready to serve (or up to 24 hours).

Preheat the oven to 450°F. Line a baking sheet with parchment paper, and set a metal wire rack over a second baking sheet.

Toss the potatoes with 5 tablespoons of the olive oil, and season liberally with salt. Place on the prepared baking sheet, arranging in a single layer. Bake, tossing occasionally, for 20 to 25 minutes, until fork-tender and golden brown.

Meanwhile, heat the remaining 2 tablespoons of the olive oil in a small skillet over medium heat. Add the panko, tarragon, garlic, lemon zest, and Parmesan, and cook, stirring, for 2 to 3 minutes, until the panko is light golden brown. Transfer to a plate and season with salt and pepper to taste.

Put the flour and a pinch of salt in a shallow bowl or cake pan. In a second shallow bowl or cake pan, beat together the eggs and mustard. Set the plate of breadcrumbs nearby. Working with one piece of fish at a time, dredge the fish in the flour, then dip in the egg mixture, turning to coat, and then into the breadcrumbs, turning to coat. Arrange the fish in a single layer on the wire rack set over the baking sheet, and bake until just cooked through, 7 to 9 minutes.

Transfer the fish and chips to a serving dish, and serve with the tartar sauce alongside.

Fish Cakes with Tarragon Aioli

For the fish cakes

1 pound haddock or cod

1½ cups whole milk

Sea salt

3 large russet potatoes, peeled and cut into ¾-inch cubes

4 tablespoons unsalted butter, divided

Freshly ground black pepper

2 tablespoons finely chopped celery (about ⅓ stalk)

½ medium white onion

2 garlic cloves, minced

1½ teaspoons finely chopped summer savory

1 teaspoon Worcestershire sauce

1 teaspoon Dijon mustard

Zest of 1 lemon

3 large eggs, divided

1¼ cups panko breadcrumbs

¼ cup grapeseed oil or other neutral oil

For the aioli

1 egg yolk, at room temperature

1 teaspoon Dijon mustard

1 garlic clove, mashed to a paste with a pinch of salt

1 tablespoon freshly squeezed lemon juice

½ cup extra-virgin olive oil

½ cup grapeseed oil or other neutral oil

1½ tablespoons finely chopped fresh tarragon

1 tablespoon minced fresh chives

Sea salt and freshly ground black pepper

Fish cakes are another classic Maritime specialty. Because the fish and potatoes are both bland, I like to season my fish cakes generously with savory Worcestershire sauce, Dijon mustard, and plenty of lemon zest. Note that the cakes should be refrigerated for one hour before you plan to cook them, but if it's more convenient for your schedule, they can be made up to six hours ahead (cover them with plastic wrap). Pan-fry them just before serving so they're hot and crisp. If you don't have time to make aioli from scratch, you can dress up store-bought mayonnaise with some finely chopped fresh tarragon, a bit of minced garlic, and a generous squeeze of lemon juice.

Make the Fish Cakes: Place the fish in a shallow dish, and pour the milk over. Cover and refrigerate overnight (or about 12 hours).

Transfer the fish and milk to a medium saucepan over medium heat, season with a pinch of salt, and bring to a gentle simmer. Cook until the fish flakes easily with a fork, about 6 to 7 minutes. Remove the fish from the milk with a slotted spoon (discard the milk) and set aside.

Put the potatoes in a large saucepan and add cold water to cover by a few inches. Bring to a boil over high heat, generously salt the water, and cook the potatoes until fork-tender, about 10 to 12 minutes. Drain and pass through a ricer into a clean bowl (alternatively, you can transfer to a bowl and mash with a handheld potato masher). Add 3 tablespoons of the butter, stirring so the butter melts, and then season to taste with salt and pepper. Flake the fish with a fork and add to the bowl with the potato.

Heat the remaining 1 tablespoon of the butter in a small skillet over medium heat. Add the celery, onion, and a pinch of salt, and cook, stirring occasionally, until softened and translucent, about 6 to 8 minutes. Add the vegetables to the bowl with the potato-fish mixture. Stir in the garlic, savory, Worcestershire sauce, mustard, lemon zest, and 1 egg, and mix well.

Line a large baking sheet with parchment paper. Divide the mixture into 8 thick, burger-sized fish cakes, each about 1½ inches thick, and place them on the prepared baking sheet. Cover and refrigerate for 1 hour.

Make the Aioli: In a medium bowl, whisk the egg yolk, mustard, and garlic paste until the yolk turns pale and slightly fluffy. Whisk in the lemon juice. Drop by drop at first and then in a slow and steady stream, drizzle in the olive oil and grapeseed oil while constantly whisking until the aioli is thick and emulsified. (If you add the oil too quickly, the aioli won't thicken, so take care to add it drop by drop at first until it begins to thicken, and then in a slow, steady stream after that. A measuring cup with a spout can help control the flow of oil.) Whisk in the tarragon and chives, and season with salt and pepper to taste. If your aioli is too thick and appears greasy, whisk in a drop or two of warm water to loosen and smooth it.

recipe continues

Finish the Fish Cakes: Remove the fish cakes from the refrigerator. In a shallow pie plate or low bowl, whisk the remaining 2 eggs. In a second pie plate or low bowl, pour your breadcrumbs and season with a pinch of salt. Working one at a time, dip a fish cake first in beaten eggs, turning to coat, then into the breadcrumbs, turning to coat all over. Return the breaded fish cake to the baking sheet, and repeat with the remaining fish cakes.

Heat the grapeseed oil in a high-sided skillet over medium heat until the oil is shimmering. Working in batches as necessary, fry the fish cakes, turning once, until golden brown, about 2 to 3 minutes per side. Transfer to a serving platter and serve with the aioli alongside.

Sriracha Maple Salmon with Avocado Pineapple Salsa

For the salmon

¼ cup pure maple syrup

3 tablespoons soy sauce

1 tablespoon rice vinegar

1 tablespoon sriracha

1 tablespoon sesame oil

3 garlic cloves, minced

1 tablespoon grated fresh ginger

Zest of 1 lime

1 skin-on salmon fillet
(about 3 pounds)

For the salsa

1 small pineapple, peeled, cored, and sliced into rounds

1 large ripe avocado, peeled, cored, and diced

½ cup finely chopped red onion

¼ cup finely chopped fresh cilantro, plus more for garnish

2 tablespoons freshly squeezed lime juice

1½ teaspoons apple cider vinegar

Sea salt and freshly ground black pepper

For serving

1 teaspoon toasted sesame seeds

1 lime, cut into wedges

I adore this recipe! This salmon has an irresistible balance of spicy and sweet, much like teriyaki, and is topped with a fresh, bright pineapple salsa (though, if you want to streamline the recipe, the fish is brilliant on its own, too). Note that the fish needs to marinate for at least 8 hours, so plan ahead. It's well worth the wait.

Prepare the Salmon: In a medium bowl, combine the syrup, soy sauce, vinegar, sriracha, sesame oil, garlic, ginger, and lime zest, and mix well. Place the salmon in an extra-large resealable freezer bag (or high-sided dish), and pour over the marinade. Close the bag (or cover the dish with plastic wrap) and refrigerate for 6 to 8 hours, turning the bag every few hours, to let the marinade work its magic. If using a high-sided dish, flip the fish every few hours.

Prepare a grill for indirect, medium-high heat cooking (see Notes on Grilling, page 187), or preheat the oven to 400°F. If baking in the oven, line a baking sheet with foil.

If grilling, remove the fish from the marinade, reserve the marinade, and lay the salmon, skin side down, on the cooler side of the grill grate and cover the grill. Cook, uncovering the grill every few minutes to brush the flesh side of the fish with some of the reserved marinade. After about 20 minutes, poke the salmon with the tip of a sharp knife. If it easily flakes, the fish is ready; if it seems underdone, cook for 5 minutes more and check again.

If baking, remove the fish from the marinade, and place skin side down on the prepared baking sheet. Brush some of the marinade all over the top, then transfer to the oven. Cook for about 20 minutes, and then poke the salmon with the tip of a sharp knife. If it easily flakes, the fish is ready; if it seems underdone, cook for 5 minutes more and check again.

Make the Salsa: Place the pineapple rounds on the hot side of the grill and cook, turning as needed with tongs, until lightly charred on both sides. Transfer to a cutting board, chop into small pieces, and transfer to a bowl. Alternatively, if making this recipe in the comfort of your warm kitchen, char the pineapple in a skillet for a few minutes, until slightly blackened on all sides.

Add the avocado, onion, and cilantro to the bowl with the pineapple. Squeeze in the lime juice, add the vinegar, and season with salt and pepper. Toss gently to combine, and season to taste with additional salt and pepper.

recipe continues

Using two large spatulas, carefully transfer the salmon from the grill (or the baking sheet, if you baked it). Garnish with some cilantro and sesame seeds, and serve with the salsa and lime wedges alongside.

Cooking Note: *Fillets of salmon typically contain pin bones, which should be removed before you cook the fish. To do so, turn a medium mixing bowl upside down and lay the fillet of fish over the bowl, skin side down (this causes the ends of the pin bones to pop out, making them more visible and easier to remove). Use your fingertips to locate the pin bones and, with a pair of tweezers, grab hold of the end of the pin bone and pull firmly to remove. Repeat until you've removed all the bones.*

Farmed versus Wild Salmon (or How to Choose Sustainable Salmon)

Growing up a stone's throw from the mighty Miramichi River, salmon has been a beloved ingredient my whole life. New Brunswick is home to some of the best salmon fishing on the planet, and folks travel from all parts of the globe to spend time wading waist deep in our Maritime waters. In recent years, however, the wild local salmon population has almost vanished. This isn't a challenge unique to the Maritimes but a global issue. Overfishing, climate change, and pollution have led to the global population decline of one of the world's most consumed seafood products.

Unlike farmed salmon, which are mostly raised in net pens in the ocean close to shore, wild salmon are also seasonal, making its availability even more limited (though frozen wild salmon is a great option). Though, thanks to conservation efforts, the wild population is rebounding, if everyone decides to eat wild salmon all the time, the natural fishery will collapse. I suggest making wild salmon an occasional treat. Look for Alaskan salmon, where the runs are healthy and well managed. If you're looking for a comparable fish that's more abundant, a good substitute is arctic char.

It can be hard for even the most conscientious consumer to make good choices when it comes to seafood, especially salmon. Salmon, found in both the northern Atlantic and northern Pacific oceans, once spawned in rivers in North America, Asia, and Europe. But climate change, the damming of rivers, and pollution have all conspired to distress and destroy the spawning grounds. Overfishing has also taken its toll. To meet demand for salmon, fish farms have cropped up, particularly in Norway and Chile. The fish—in this case Atlantic salmon—are raised in open net pens in the ocean. And while that might seem on the face of it to be a great solution to the problem of a distressed wild salmon population, there are problems. The farmed fish are fed ground-up wild fish, which depletes that stock that the wild salmon depend on too. In addition, most farmed fish are treated with antibiotics. And the antibiotic residue, along with the fish feces, contaminate the ocean. And, of course, farmed fish occasionally escape, where they can spread disease and challenge the local population of wild fish.

However, not all salmon farms are created equal. Change is happening. There are fish farmers who are committed to minimizing the negative impact of farming and raising the fish responsibly. The Aquaculture Stewardship Council (asc-aqua.org) is an independent nonprofit that certifies farms that are farming fish responsibly. And land-raised aquaculture (my preference for sourcing year-round farmed salmon for my kitchen and to serve my family) is changing the salmon landscape, with new and exciting sustainable, traceable, microplastic-free, antibiotic- and hormone-free salmon becoming available and accessible in the marketplace. If you're considering buying farmed salmon, you can ask if it's ASC certified.

In general, however, wild salmon sourced from Alaska, where the population is well managed, is still the choice, both from a sustainability and a flavor standpoint. It is also, I'll admit, a lot more expensive than farmed salmon. So I choose to eat it in moderation, as a special occasion treat rather than a weekly staple.

Another useful source for information is the Monterey Bay Aquarium's Seafood Watch program (seafoodwatch.org). It gives science-based recommendations that help consumers and businesses make ocean-friendly seafood choices. The website (and app, which is especially handy when you're at the fish counter trying to make choices) is easy to use and frequently updated with the latest information about the best fish to choose (and avoid).

Pan-Seared Branzino with Tomato-Caper Sauce and Creamy Polenta

For the polenta

5 cups chicken stock

1 cup polenta

½ cup heavy (35%) cream

2 tablespoons unsalted butter

½ cup grated Parmesan cheese

½ cup pecorino Romano

Zest of 1 lemon

Sea salt and freshly ground black pepper

For the branzino

4 large branzino fillets (about 1 pound), skin on, pin bones removed (see Cooking Note, page 170) or 2 whole branzinos (about 3 pounds)

Sea salt

2 tablespoons extra-virgin olive oil

1 cup cherry tomatoes, halved

½ cup pitted kalamata olives

2 garlic cloves, minced

2 tablespoons capers, rinsed and drained

¼ cup dry white wine

1 tablespoon unsalted butter

Juice of ½ lemon

2 tablespoons minced fresh basil, plus more for garnish

Branzino, also known as European bass, is a mild, flaky white fish that's incredibly versatile and can be sustainably farmed. It's often served as a whole fish, but here I opt for fillets, which are simple and quick to cook (if your fish counter only has whole branzinos, you can ask them to do the filleting for you). Because this is a mild fish, I like to serve it with a punchy tomato sauce loaded with briny capers and black olives—and creamy polenta is the ideal accompaniment.

Make the Polenta: Bring the chicken stock to a simmer, and whisk in the polenta in a slow and steady stream until completely combined. Reduce the heat to low, and let the polenta bubble away for about 30 to 35 minutes, whisking often, until silky smooth. Whisk in the cream, butter, Parmesan, pecorino, and lemon zest, and season with salt and pepper to taste. Cover and set aside to keep warm.

Prepare the Branzino: Pat the fish fillets dry with paper towel, and score the skin with a sharp knife, making three shallow cuts on a diagonal (this will help create the crispiest skin ever). Season each fillet all over with salt. If using a whole fish, trim the fins off with scissors and pat the fish dry with paper towel. Using a sharp knife, score the skin on each side of the fish as above. Season each fish on both sides.

Heat the olive oil in a nonstick skillet over medium-high heat until the oil is shimmering. Carefully add the fish to the skillet, skin side down, and cook for 3 minutes. When the skin is crisp and golden, flip and cook for an additional 45 seconds. Transfer to a serving platter, skin side up.

Add the tomatoes, olives, garlic, and capers to the hot skillet, and cook for 1 minute, stirring often. Pour in the wine, and cook until reduced by half, about 2 minutes. Stir in the butter and let it melt. Remove from the heat and add the lemon juice and basil. Spoon the tomato mixture around the fish fillets and garnish with fresh basil.

Spoon the polenta onto a serving platter, then top with the fish fillets, tomato mixture, garnish with basil, and serve.

Crispy Rainbow Trout with Fennel Barley Risotto

For the risotto

8 cups chicken stock, homemade (page 200) or store-bought

2 tablespoons extra-virgin olive oil

2 medium leeks, white and light green parts only, thinly sliced

½ medium yellow onion, finely chopped

1 large fennel bulb, diced, fronds reserved

Sea salt

4 garlic cloves, minced

1½ cups pearl barley

½ cup dry white wine

Zest and juice of 1 lemon

2 tablespoons unsalted butter

1 cup grated aged cheddar cheese

Freshly ground black pepper

¼ cup minced fresh dill, plus more for garnish

For the trout

6 skin-on rainbow trout fillets (8 ounces each), pin bones removed (see Cooking Note, page 170)

Sea salt and freshly ground black pepper

Zest of 1 lemon

1½ tablespoons minced fresh tarragon

2 tablespoons extra-virgin olive oil

1 tablespoon unsalted butter

Juice of ½ lemon

Risotto is happiness in a dish, and quite possibly the most romantic bite you could serve. It takes time, attention, and, of course, a dash of love. This recipe borrows the cooking method from risotto, but I substitute pearl barley for the arborio rice, and is the first dish I prepared on our first cooking day while filming *Restaurants on the Edge* in Muskoka, Ontario. I first toast the grains until they smell nutty, and then gradually add chicken stock, letting the grains lap up and absorb the liquid before adding more. As it cooks, the barley releases starch, so the mixture becomes exceptionally creamy and toothsome. The risotto is an excellent foil for some simple, pan-fried trout fillets. Cook the fish until the skin is super crispy, which gives it a beautiful textural contrast to the risotto.

Make the Risotto: Pour the chicken stock in a large saucepan and bring to a gentle simmer over medium-low heat.

Heat the olive oil in a large, high-sided skillet over medium heat until the oil is shimmering. Carefully add the leeks, onion, fennel, and a pinch of salt. Cook, stirring occasionally, until the vegetables are softened and translucent, 6 to 8 minutes. Add the garlic and continue cooking for 45 seconds, stirring often.

Stir in the barley and continue cooking, stirring constantly, for about 3 minutes, or until the grains are well coated in oil, aromatic, and slightly toasted. Pour in the wine and add the lemon zest, and continue stirring as the barley gently absorbs the liquid. When the wine has almost been entirely absorbed, begin adding the chicken stock, about ½ cup at a time, stirring constantly, allowing each addition of liquid to be absorbed by the barley before adding more. Continue to cook, stirring and adding additional stock as needed until the risotto is tender and creamy, 40 to 45 minutes. Taste the barley for doneness—it should still be slightly al dente.

Remove from the heat and vigorously stir in the lemon juice, butter, and cheese to combine. Taste and season with salt and pepper, and stir in the dill. Cover and set aside.

Prepare the Trout: Season the flesh side of the fillets with salt and pepper, and then coat with the lemon zest and tarragon. Heat the olive oil a large nonstick skillet over medium-high heat. Working in batches if needed, lay the fish skin side down in the skillet, and cook until the skin is crisp and golden, about 3 minutes. Flip, and continue cooking until the fish is cooked through, 2 to 3 minutes longer. Remove the skillet from the heat and add the butter to the skillet. When the butter is foaming, baste the fish with the melted butter, and then squeeze in the lemon juice.

Spoon the risotto onto individual plates. Top each with a piece of fish, skin side up, season with salt, and garnish with dill.

Grilled Halibut Tacos with Creamy Slaw and Avocado Crema

For the halibut

¼ cup grapeseed oil or other neutral oil

Zest and juice of 1 lime

1 tablespoon orange zest

1 tablespoon freshly squeezed orange juice

1 tablespoon ancho chili powder

1 jalapeño pepper, stemmed, seeded, and minced

2 garlic cloves, minced

¼ cup finely chopped fresh cilantro

Sea salt

1½ pounds halibut steaks

For the slaw

4 cups very thinly sliced green or red cabbage

1 carrot, peeled and grated

2 radishes, thinly sliced

¼ cup minced fresh cilantro

1 green onion, thinly sliced

1 tablespoon extra-virgin olive oil

1 tablespoon red wine vinegar

1 tablespoon freshly squeezed lime juice

1½ teaspoons pure maple syrup

Sea salt and freshly ground black pepper

For the crema

2 ripe avocados, halved, peeled, and pitted

1 cup sour cream

1 cup finely chopped fresh cilantro

¼ teaspoon ground cumin

Zest and juice of 2 limes

Sea salt

For serving

Warm flour tortillas, homemade (page 212) or store-bought

1 to 2 jalapeño peppers, thinly sliced

Lime wedges

Mild and lean but meaty, halibut is one of my favorite fish. It's excellent for grilling, because it doesn't fall apart on the grate and absorbs flavors well, so a quick marinating in citrus-chili-garlic gives the fish a lot of flavor without much fuss. For this shareable family-style dinner, I set out the grilled fish, a stack of warm flour tortillas, a bowl of crunchy, creamy slaw, and another of avocado crema, and invite my guests to customize their own taco. Fun, a breeze to prepare, and entirely delicious.

Prepare the Halibut: In a medium bowl, stir together the grapeseed oil, lime zest, lime juice, orange zest, orange juice, chili powder, jalapeño, garlic, and cilantro, mix well, and season with salt to taste. Place the halibut in a shallow skillet, pour over the marinade, and let sit at room temperature for 20 minutes.

Preheat a grill for direct, high-heat grilling (see Notes on Grilling, page 187), and lightly oil the grill grate.

Make the Slaw: In a large bowl, combine the cabbage, carrot, radishes, cilantro, green onion, olive oil, vinegar, lime, and syrup, and toss well to mix. Season to taste with salt and pepper and set aside.

Make the Crema: In a blender or food processor combine the avocados, sour cream, cilantro, cumin, lime zest, lime juice, and a generous pinch of salt. Blend until silky smooth. Season to taste with additional salt. Transfer to a serving bowl.

Grill the Halibut: Remove the halibut from the marinade (discard the marinade) and place on the preheated grill. Grill the fish, turning once with a large spatula, for about 5 to 6 minutes per side, until the fish is golden brown and flakes easily and an instant-read thermometer inserted in the thickest part reaches 135°F. Resist the urge to flip the fish too soon, as the flesh may stick to the grill; once it is browned it should pull away from the grate without sticking. Transfer to a plate and let rest for 5 minutes (the residual heat will continue cooking the fish to a perfectly done 145°F as it rests).

With a fork, flake the fish into pieces, discarding skin and bone. Serve with the slaw, avocado crema, tortillas, jalapeños, and lime wedges.

Grilled Lobster 101

When I say I love lobster, I really mean it—I even inked a very present lobster tattoo on my forearm. Here in New Brunswick, our incredible fishermen sell their catch at local fish shops and markets, and even out of the back of half-ton trucks parked in parking lots (look for the handwritten sign and a long line). What a delicious life it is!

Aside from lobster rolls, my other favorite way of preparing these special crustaceans is grilled and then slathered with a flavorful compound butter. The contrast of the smokiness from the grill and the sweet lobster meat is perfect, and because it's not steamed or boiled, the flavor is absolutely undiluted. The method is simple but requires a tad bit of courage. Killing a live lobster, if you've never done it, seems a little scary. Fear not! This method is the quickest and most humane way to do it.

Prepare a grill for direct, high-heat grilling (see Notes on Grilling, page 187).

Using a very sharp knife (and all of your courage), split the lobster in half lengthwise: Lay the lobster belly-down on a cutting board and insert a large, sharp knife into the head section with the blade pointing forward. Press down firmly to split the head in half. Carefully reinsert the knife into the head, this time with the blade pointing toward the tail, and split the rest of the lobster in half. Press down firmly on the flat side of the knife to ensure you've cut all the way through, and separate the lobster into two halves. Scoop out and discard the tomalley (green and yellow stuff), and then break off the claws. Rub the lobster halves and claws with olive oil and season all over with salt and pepper.

Place the lobster halves, flesh side down, with the claws on the hottest part of your grill, and cook for 3 minutes, until slightly charred. Flip and dot the lobster meat with some of the compound butter of choice (page 182). Continue cooking for 5 to 6 minutes, or until the lobster flesh is tender and cooked through.

Transfer to a platter and serve with extra melted compound butter and lemon wedges.

MY COMPOUND BUTTER HOLY TRINITY

Compound butters are a simple way to add a Mariana Trench–depth of flavor to almost any dish. I make them in advance, rolling the flavored butter into a log, and store in my freezer. Then, when I want to use them, I simply slice off as many disks as I need—perfect for plopping on a steak as it rests or on a piece of steamed or grilled fish, or dropping into a soup or pasta dish. When I want a large quantity of the butter (like, for example, when I'm serving it with grilled lobster), I can melt it all to serve alongside. The recipes below make enough butter for six to eight grilled lobsters, but you can make a half-batch if you need less.

Caribbean-Inspired Compound Butter MAKES ABOUT 1 CUP

1 cup (2 sticks) unsalted butter, softened

3 garlic cloves, minced

2 tablespoons minced fresh cilantro

2 tablespoons finely minced fresh chives

1 tablespoon finely chopped fresh ginger

Zest and juice of 1 lime

½ teaspoon curry powder

½ teaspoon ground turmeric

¼ teaspoon cayenne powder

Sea salt and freshly ground black pepper

Combine all the ingredients in a medium bowl and mix until well combined. Transfer to a sheet of parchment paper or plastic wrap and, using the parchment or plastic as an aid, shape and roll your butter into a log, grip the ends, and twist them in opposite directions to secure the roll. Refrigerate until firm or for up to 3 days, or freeze for up to 3 months.

Garlic Herb Compound Butter MAKES ABOUT 1 CUP

1 cup (2 sticks) unsalted butter, softened

1 tablespoon finely chopped fresh flat-leaf parsley

1 tablespoon finely chopped fresh tarragon

1 tablespoon minced shallot

3 garlic cloves, minced

1 tablespoon lemon zest

Sea salt and freshly ground black pepper

Combine all the ingredients in a medium bowl and mix until well combined. Transfer to a sheet of parchment paper or plastic wrap and, using the parchment or plastic as an aid, shape and roll your butter into a log, grip the ends, and twist them in opposite directions to secure the roll. Refrigerate until firm or for up to 3 days, or freeze for up to 3 months.

Smoky Anchovy Butter MAKES ABOUT 1 CUP

1 cup (2 sticks) unsalted butter, softened

4 garlic cloves, minced

1 teaspoon smoked paprika

1 can (2 ounces) oil-packed anchovies, drained and minced to a paste

⅓ cup finely chopped fresh dill

Zest of 1 lemon

Sea salt and freshly ground black pepper

Combine all the ingredients in a medium bowl, and mix until well combined. Transfer to a sheet of parchment paper or plastic wrap and, using the parchment or plastic as an aid, shape and roll your butter into a log, grip the ends, and twist them in opposite directions to secure the roll. Refrigerate until firm or for up to 3 days, or freeze for up to 3 months.

Aboiteau-Style Clambake

1 bottle (25 fluid ounces) dry white wine

4 cups fish stock

8 garlic cloves, minced

Zest of 2 lemons

2 tablespoons Old Bay seasoning

Sea salt

3 pounds skin-on new potatoes

8 live lobsters (1¼ pounds each)

2 leeks, white and light green parts only, trimmed and cut into 2-inch lengths

8 ears corn, shucked and halved

1 small bunch fresh thyme, stems tied together

1 small bunch fresh tarragon, stems tied together

2 bay leaves

3 pounds steamer clams

1½ pounds mussels

Freshly ground black pepper

Lemon wedges, for serving

Melted unsalted butter, for serving

Crusty bread, for sopping up all that deliciousness

This is a festive summertime feast for a crowd. I took inspiration from the classic clambakes prepared both at the wharf restaurant and on the surrounding beaches of Aboiteau Beach (and up and down the Acadian Shores) in New Brunswick, where I get together with friends and family for an all-day cooking experience. It begins by digging a hole in the sand, lining it with rocks, building a big fire, and, when it has cooked down to coals, layering in a panoply of seafood and vegetables to cook in the subterranean oven. It's a magical experience, and if you ever have a day to spare, you should try it!

Recognizing that not all of us have that kind of time—or access to a beach, for that matter—I developed this simpler clambake method. Because of the volume of ingredients called for, I think it's easiest to cook this over a live fire (with a grate set over it on which to set the pot), or over a freestanding propane burner (like the kind you might own if you've ever deep-fried a turkey). That will give you the fire power you need to cook this quickly and easily. When it's done cooking, you can pile all the ingredients on platters or pile them directly onto a newspaper-lined table for an al fresco feast.

In a 50-quart stockpot (get the absolute largest stockpot you can find, friends) over high heat combine the wine, stock, garlic, lemon zest, and Old Bay, season with salt to taste, and bring to a rolling boil. Be sure to taste here as Old Bay is quite salty (and delicious). Add the potatoes, return to a boil, and cook for 5 minutes.

Add the lobster, cover the pot, and cook for 8 minutes. Add the leeks, corn, thyme, tarragon, bay leaves, clams, and mussels. Season with a few big pinches of salt and pepper, cover, and cook for 8 to 10 minutes, until the mussels and clams open and the corn is tender.

With tongs and a large spider, remove the potatoes, lobsters, leeks, corn, clams, and mussels from the pot (discarding any mussels or clams that haven't opened), and divide among two large serving platters. Serve right away, with lemon wedges, melted butter, loads of crusty bread, and lots of napkins alongside.

Notes on Grilling

DIRECT GRILLING

When a recipe calls for direct grilling, this means that you're grilling the food directly over the fire. This method is ideal for smaller, quick-cooking items (think burgers, kebabs, and vegetables), which will cook through and brown on the exterior at approximately the same rate.

If Using a Gas Grill: Open the lid, press the ignition, turn all burners to high, close the lid, and wait 10 minutes or so for the grill to get hot. Then adjust the burners for the temperature range you need. As you cook, keep the lid closed as much as possible.

If Using a Charcoal Grill: My favorite way to start a charcoal fire is the chimney starter. Stuff a few pieces of crumpled newspaper in its base, and fill with enough charcoal to cover the cooking grate in a single layer—usually to the top of the chimney for a standard kettle grill. Set the chimney on the firegrate (the bottom grate) and open the vents underneath the grill. Ignite the paper and let the fire burn until all the charcoal ignites, 15 to 20 minutes. Protecting your hands, dump the charcoal onto the firegrate and spread it out with tongs. Then put the cooking grate in place to preheat and let the coals burn to the heat specified in your recipe—usually 5 to 10 minutes for high, longer for medium to low. If you can spare the grill space, leave about one-quarter of the firegrate clear of coals. This will give you a cool zone where you can temporarily move any foods that start to get too brown. If you need to reduce the fire's temperature when you're grilling, partially close vents in the lid and at firegrate level. (You reduce the oxygen that feeds the fire, which will slow its burn.)

HOW TO GAUGE THE HEAT

For direct, very high–heat grilling (550°F to 650°F), you should be able to hold your hand 5 inches above the cooking grate for only 1 to 2 seconds. For direct, high–heat grilling (450°F to 550°F), you should be able to hold your hand 5 inches above the cooking grate for only 2 to 4 seconds. For direct, medium–heat grilling (350°F to 450°F), you should be able to hold your hand 5 inches above the cooking grate for only 5 to 7 seconds. And for direct, low–heat cooking (250°F to 350°F), you should be able to hold your hand 5 inches above the cooking grate for 8 to 10 seconds. With a charcoal grill, temperature fluctuations are to be expected, so check the temperature frequently, adding coals (or moving food to a cooler part of the grill) as needed.

INDIRECT GRILLING
(ALSO CALLED MULTI ZONE GRILLING)

When a recipe calls for indirect grilling, this means that the food is not cooked directly over the fire, but instead is cooked by the radiant heat from a fire that burns adjacent. This gentler method is well-suited to larger cuts of meat, which take longer to cook, and to fattier cuts, which would drip and cause flare-ups if cooked over direct heat.

If Using a Gas Grill: Set a drip pan on one burner, ignite all the burners, turn them to high, close the grill lid, and wait 10 minutes for the grill to preheat. Turn off the burner with the drip pan on it and adjust the other burners until you have the temperature you need. Set the food over the drip pan, and grill with the lid closed.

If Using a Charcoal Grill: Use the instructions for lighting a charcoal grill (page 188), using about two-thirds the amount of charcoal you'd use for direct grilling. Dump out the coals and arrange them on both sides of the firegrate, leaving the center clear. Place a drip pan in the center, and then let the coals burn down to the desired temperature, 5 to 10 minutes. Place the food on the grate directly above the drip pan and cover the grill, leaving the vents open. If you're cooking for more than 30 minutes, you'll need to add coals periodically, about 10 briquettes every 30 minutes. Uncover the grill, add the briquettes, and leave uncovered for a few minutes to allow the added charcoal to light, and then recover. If the temperature gets too high, adjust it by partially closing the vents in the lid and on the bottom of the grill.

If Using a Pellet Grill: Another great choice for indirect grilling is a pellet grill (it happens to be my absolute favorite). The grill uses hardwood pellets (you can choose the hardwood, depending on what you're grilling), ignited by an electric starter. You set the desired temperature and time, and let the warm, smoky air circulate around the food, much the way a convection oven works. In fact, pellet grills are so versatile and precise, they can be used to "bake" things, too. They're ideal for hands-off, low-stress, precise, indirect grilling. And because pellet grills are temperature regulated, when you set your grill to a temp, it stays there (unlike other forms of grilling), so literally anything you would normally make in your traditional oven, you can now infuse with wood-fired flavor on your grill. Yes, please! Perfect food, every time. Trust me, get a pellet grill.

CHOOSING CHARCOAL

If grilling with charcoal, you have two widely available options: briquettes or hardwood charcoal. Briquettes, made of crushed charcoal (and, sometimes, coal) light quickly and burn longer than hardwood charcoal. Just avoid briquettes that have lighter fluid added, as it can give food a chemical flavor. Hardwood charcoal (also sometimes called lump charcoal), by contrast, takes longer to light but burns very hot. It also loses heat more quickly, so if you're grilling something that will take longer than 20 to 30 minutes, you'll want to use a generous amount.

An Omnivore's Delight

Meaty Mains
for Every Occasion

There's a special magic in an expertly cooked medium-rare steak, juicy and tender smoked chicken, or fall-off-the-bone braised pork. A perfect bite. An omnivore's delight. In a word, it's art. I've always been an adventurous eater, and as I've had the good fortune to travel across the globe over the past two decades, I've had the privilege to try unique and exciting dishes from Nairobi to New York, and Stockholm to Santo Domingo. And though we may not be able to taste every dish in its homeland, we can travel the globe through our kitchens, through flavor, and through stories shared at the family table. In this chapter, you'll find meaty recipes inspired by my travels, as well as some iconic American favorites, including burgers and pulled pork.

I don't want to get too preachy about it, but I do think it's vitally important that we consider where our meat comes from, and how it's treated and raised. Yes, I do still eat meat, but I only really enjoy it when I know it has been raised humanely, without antibiotics, having spent its life doing the things animals like to do. But, you say, that meat is expensive! I agree. But it also reflects the real cost of doing things the right way. And the right way is always the best way. Because I've decided these are my values when it comes to eating meat, I'm willing to pay more. But because it costs more, I also eat it less frequently, which is a net gain for my health and the health of the planet.

In the recipes that follow, I've tried to cover the bases, from simple, quick weeknight meals (meatballs, and sandwiches!) to feasts that I'll only make for a crowd, or a special occasion (like turkey roulade or bistecca alla fiorentina). Whether you eat meat once a day, once a week, or once a year, these stellar preparations will help you make the most of it.

Grilled Teriyaki Chicken

2 tablespoons cornstarch

1½ cups soy sauce

½ cup packed dark brown sugar

¾ cup mirin

3 garlic cloves, minced

1 tablespoon grated fresh ginger

1 tablespoon sriracha, plus more for serving

3 pounds boneless, skinless chicken thighs

2 bunches broccolini

2 tablespoons extra-virgin olive oil

Sea salt

2 green onions, sliced, for garnish

2 teaspoons toasted sesame seeds, for garnish

1 lime, cut into wedges, for serving

Steamed jasmine rice, for serving

No one can resist this lacquered, sticky, salty-sweet chicken. It's a perennial takeout favorite that is, as it turns out, quite easy to replicate at home. Because the marinade contains a lot of sugar, you need to take some care when grilling so the exterior doesn't burn before the meat is cooked through. I like to cook the chicken over indirect heat, moving it on and off the hotter part of the grill so it gets nicely caramelized but doesn't char. If you're looking for a side dish to serve with the chicken, try the Spicy Gochujang Green Beans (page 60), some simply beautiful grilled broccolini, or serve it with Flavor-Bomb Pickles (page 215) alongside.

In a large bowl whisk together the cornstarch, soy sauce, brown sugar, mirin, garlic, ginger, and sriracha. Add the chicken and stir well to coat. Cover and marinate for at least 4 hours or up to 24 hours.

When ready to cook, preheat a grill for indirect, medium–heat grilling (see Notes on Grilling, page 187).

Remove the chicken from the marinade, reserving the marinade, and place the chicken on the cooler side of the grill. Cook for about 20 minutes, flipping halfway through, and moving the pieces on and off the hotter part of the grill, until caramelized and an instant-read thermometer inserted in the thickest part of a thigh reaches 165°F. When 10 minutes of cooking time remain for the chicken, toss the broccolini with the olive oil, season with salt, and add to the grill alongside the chicken. Grill, turning often, until charred and tender.

Meanwhile, pour the reserved marinade into a small saucepan and bring to a boil over medium-high heat. Cook for 2 to 3 minutes, reduce the heat to medium-low, and cook until thickened.

Remove the chicken from the grill and let rest for 5 minutes. Slice into thin strips and pour the reduced marinade over top. Transfer to a platter and pile the broccolini alongside. Garnish with the green onions and toasted sesame seeds, and serve with lime wedges and rice alongside.

Cooking Note: *If it's a bleak midwinter night, and firing the grill isn't a comfortable option, this can most certainly be made in the comfort of your indoor kitchen. You may lose that delicious smoky char, but gain the ability to not freeze your face off. Simply heat 1 tablespoon of a neutral oil in a large skillet over medium heat. Working in batches as necessary, add the chicken (reserving the marinade per the above instructions) and cook for 5 minutes. Flip and continue cooking for an additional 5 to 7 minutes, until crisp, caramelized, and cooked through to an internal temperature of 165°F. Finish per the above instructions and enjoy!*

Berbere-Kissed Braised Chicken and Lentils

4 large bone-in chicken leg quarters (thigh and drumstick) (about 3½ to 4 pounds)

2 tablespoons extra-virgin olive oil

3 tablespoons berbere spice, divided (see Cooking Note)

Zest of 1 lime

Sea salt

¼ cup grapeseed or other neutral oil

1 large yellow onion, finely chopped

1 tablespoon tomato paste

3 garlic cloves, minced

1-inch piece fresh ginger, peeled and minced

2 tablespoons minced fresh cilantro stems

½ teaspoon ground cumin

1 teaspoon smoked paprika

2 Roma tomatoes, cored and diced

1 cup dry beluga (black) lentils

3 cups chicken stock, homemade (page 200) or store-bought

Juice of 1 lime

2 tablespoons coconut oil

Freshly ground black pepper

¼ cup heavy (35%) cream, for drizzling

1 bird's eye or Thai chili, stemmed and thinly sliced

¼ cup fresh cilantro, chopped

Lime wedges, for serving

Steamed rice, injera, naan, or pita bread, for serving

In summer 2018, I traveled with World Vision Canada to Addis Ababa, Ethiopia, and left filled with inspiration! Mealtime in Ethiopia is precious, celebrated, and communal, and Ethiopian food is one of the most vibrant cuisines on planet earth. And the coffee! Oh my!

For this simple braise, I season pieces of bone-in chicken with berbere, an Ethiopian spice blend containing chilies, garlic, fenugreek, and a handful of warm spices, such as allspice and cinnamon. The chicken gets browned and finishes cooking on a bed of spiced black lentils, which become flavored with the chicken fat and juices. Yum! I like to serve this with store-bought injera, a spongy, sour Ethiopian flatbread that's made from teff flour. If you have an Ethiopian grocery store near you (or even an Ethiopian restaurant you can order takeout from), you might do the same. If not, you can substitute naan or pita, or skip the bread altogether.

In a medium bowl, combine the chicken, olive oil, 1½ tablespoons of the berbere spice, and lime zest, and season well with salt. Massage until completely coated. Cover with plastic wrap and refrigerate for at least 1 hour (up to 4 hours).

Preheat the oven (or grill) to 400°F.

Heat the grapeseed oil in a large Dutch oven over medium heat until the oil is shimmering. Working in batches as necessary, add the chicken skin side down, and cook until the skin is golden and starting to crisp, about 3 to 4 minutes. Remove and set aside.

Next, add the onion, season with a pinch of salt, and cook until softened and translucent, about 6 to 8 minutes. Stir in the remaining 1½ tablespoons of the berbere spice, tomato paste, garlic, ginger, cilantro stems, cumin, and paprika. Cook, stirring often, for 2 minutes.

Add the tomatoes, lentils, stock, lime juice, and coconut oil, season with salt and several generous cracks of black pepper, and bring to a boil. Nestle the chicken legs, skin side up, on top of the bed of lentils, and transfer to the oven. Cook until the sauce has thickened, the lentils are tender, and the chicken is cooked through (an instant-read thermometer inserted in the thickest part of the kitchen should register 165°F), about 45 minutes to 1 hour. Taste and adjust the seasoning.

Drizzle over the cream, and garnish with sliced chilies (if you're feeling extra spicy) and cilantro. Serve with lime wedges and steamed rice or injera alongside.

Cooking Note: *You can order berbere online or find it at well-stocked grocery stores. It's a wonderful addition to your spice cabinet, adding lots of flavor with no effort.*

Chicken Fricot

1 whole chicken (about 3½ to 4 pounds) or 2 bone-in chicken drumsticks, 2 bone-in chicken thighs, and 2 bone-in chicken breasts, halved crosswise

Sea salt

3 tablespoons unsalted butter

1 large white onion, diced

4 large carrots, peeled and diced

3 celery stalks, diced

4 garlic cloves, minced

6 cups chicken stock, homemade (page 200) or store-bought

6 cups water

1½ tablespoons summer savory, divided

2 pounds russet potatoes, scrubbed and diced

Freshly ground black pepper

1 cup all-purpose flour

1 tablespoon baking powder

½ tablespoon lemon zest

Chopped fresh flat-leaf parsley, for garnish

Cooking Note: *This recipe freezes perfectly, and I always have a batch or two at the ready in case a cold unexpectedly strikes. Make just the chicken stew, let cool to room temperature, and transfer to plastic freezer storage bags. When you're ready to eat the stew, thaw the chicken mixture and bring to a simmer, and then make the dumplings and add them to the simmering stew. It's more economical to begin with a whole chicken and butcher it into 8 pieces (save the back for chicken stock— see page 200), though if you prefer you can also buy chicken pieces.*

Chicken fricot is happiness in a bowl. This Acadian version of chicken and dumplings is the height of cold-weather comfort food. Though I'm not Acadian myself, I've had the privilege to grow up alongside that incredible community. This is a humble, nostalgia-packed recipe that folks from my part of the world enjoy when feeling a tad under the weather, when a nor'easter rears its wintery head, or when we just want a taste of home. My version steers slightly away from the original, adding garlic and lemon, and will become part of your recipe repertoire for years to come.

Cut the chicken into 8 pieces (see Cooking Note), and season all over with salt.

Heat a large Dutch oven or pot over medium heat and melt the butter. When the butter has melted, and working in batches as necessary, add the chicken pieces skin side down and cook until the skin is golden brown, 7 to 8 minutes. Flip and continue cooking until a beautiful sunshine color develops on the second side, 3 to 4 minutes. With tongs, transfer the chicken to a rimmed plate.

Add the onions, carrots, and celery to the pot, season with a pinch of salt, and cook until softened and translucent, about 6 to 8 minutes. Stir in the garlic and cook for 45 seconds, until fragrant.

Add the stock, water, chicken, 1 tablespoon of the summer savory, and a pinch of salt, and bring to a boil. Reduce the heat to medium, and cook until the chicken is tender, about 30 to 35 minutes. Add the potatoes, and continue cooking for about 12 to 15 minutes, or until the potatoes are just fork-tender. Remove from the heat.

Using a slotted spoon, remove the chicken and transfer to a cutting board. When cool enough to handle, shred the meat with 2 forks, discarding the skin and bones, and then return the meat to the broth. Skim and discard the fat on top of the broth. Taste and adjust the seasoning as necessary, adding more salt or pepper.

In a medium bowl, combine the flour, baking powder, the remaining ½ tablespoon of the summer savory, and lemon zest, season with salt, and mix well. While constantly stirring, gradually add about ½ to ¾ cup of water to the flour mixture until the dough comes together.

Return the chicken stew to the stove and bring to a simmer over medium heat. When simmering, drop tablespoon-sized portions of the dough into the fricot, cover, and cook for 7 minutes, or until the little dough balls are cooked through.

Divide your fricot into individual bowls, garnish with parsley, and enter a wonderful world of Acadian comfort.

My Secret-Weapon Chicken Stock

4 pounds chicken bones

1 pound chicken wings

Sea salt and freshly ground black pepper

2 large yellow onions, chopped

1 large leek, white and light green parts only, roughly chopped

3 carrots, sliced

2 celery stalks, chopped

2 large parsnips, chopped

1 head of garlic, halved

6 sprigs fresh thyme

6 sprigs fresh rosemary

2 bay leaves

½ bunch fresh flat-leaf parsley

1 tablespoon toasted fennel seeds

1½ tablespoons whole black peppercorns

Yes, of course you can buy chicken stock at the grocery store, and there's no shame in doing so. But making your own is simple, and the resulting golden broth is incredibly flavorful. You can start with raw chicken bones, as instructed by the recipe, but you can also save up bones from roasted chickens, reserving them in the freezer until you have enough. If you're starting with bones that have been cooked once, they won't need to be roasted as long as if you were starting with raw bones; just roast them until lightly browned.

Preheat the oven to 350°F (bonus points if you do this on a grill, as it adds beautiful smoky notes to your stock). Lightly oil 2 large rimmed baking sheets.

Place the chicken bones and chicken wings on one of the baking sheets and lightly season with salt and pepper. Roast, turning halfway through, for about 1½ hours or until beautifully caramelized. Be sure not to burn the bones, as it will add a bitter note to your stock.

When you have 30 minutes remaining in your roasting time, place the onions, leeks, carrots, celery, and parsnips on the second baking sheet, lightly season with salt (see Cooking Note) and pepper, and roast alongside your chicken bones for the remaining 30 minutes.

In a large stockpot combine the roasted chicken bones, chicken wings, and vegetables, and add 3½ quarts of water. Add the garlic, thyme, rosemary, bay leaves, parsley, fennel seeds, and peppercorns, and bring to a boil over high heat. Reduce the heat to low and let the stock slowly simmer and bubble away for 4 hours. Every 30 minutes or so, skim the scum from the top of your stock and discard.

Pour the stock through a fine-mesh sieve into a clean pot or bowl. Let cool to room temperature, pour into an airtight container, and refrigerate until ready to use. The stock will keep, refrigerated, for 1 week. For longer storage, transfer the cooled stock into plastic resealable freezer bags, lay flat on a baking sheet, freeze until solid, and stack in the freezer for up to 6 months.

Cooking Note: *You'll notice that I use just the tiniest amount of salt here, as I prefer to season the stock to taste when I'm using it as a base in other recipes, but feel free to season to taste as you prefer, friends.*

Thai-Style Red Curry Turkey Meatballs

For the meatballs

1 pound ground turkey
(preferably dark meat)

1 tablespoon very finely chopped lemongrass

1 tablespoon grated fresh ginger

4 garlic cloves, minced

3 makrut lime leaves, thinly sliced
(or zest of 1 lime, in a pinch)

2 bird's eye or Thai chilies,
stemmed, seeded, and very
finely chopped (or less, if you're
feeling less spicy)

2 tablespoons minced fresh
cilantro

2 teaspoons pure maple syrup

1 tablespoon fish sauce

¾ cup panko breadcrumbs

1 large egg, lightly whisked

For the curry

2 tablespoons grapeseed oil
or other neutral oil

1 tablespoon minced fresh ginger

3 garlic cloves, minced

1 tablespoon minced basil stems

6 tablespoons prepared
red curry paste

3½ cups full-fat coconut milk

1 tablespoon lime zest

2 tablespoons fish sauce

2 teaspoons pure maple syrup

1 cup snow peas

For serving

½ cup fresh basil

Cooked jasmine rice

2 limes, cut into wedges

These aromatic little meatballs are a double threat: simple to prepare and righteously delicious. Ground turkey is quite lean and—let's face it—a bit bland. To counteract the first problem, I opt for dark meat turkey, which has a bit more fat, and therefore a bit more flavor, and punch up the aromatics, seasoning the meat with lemongrass, garlic, lime leaf, chilies, cilantro, and fish sauce. For the coconut curry sauce, use a good-quality store-bought red curry paste, but be sure to taste it, as some brands can be spicier than others, and you may find you want to use less (or more!). Serve this with steamed rice for soaking up the saucy goodness.

Make the Meatballs: In a large bowl, combine the turkey, lemongrass, ginger, garlic, lime leaves, chilies, cilantro, syrup, fish sauce, bread-crumbs, and egg. Mix well. Divide and shape in heaped tablespoon golf ball–sized meatballs. Note: If you're a planner (I'm not, so kudos to you), these meatballs can be prepped in advance and stored in the fridge overnight to cut down on prep time at dinner.

Make the Curry: Heat the grapeseed oil in a large, high-sided skillet over medium heat until the oil is shimmering. Working in batches as necessary, add the meatballs and brown on all sides, about 3 to 4 minutes. Remove with a slotted spoon and set aside.

Add the ginger, garlic, and basil stems, and cook for 2 minutes, stirring often. Stir in the red curry paste, coconut milk, and lime zest. Add the meatballs to the sauce and bring to a boil. Reduce the heat to medium-low and let that goodness simmer away until the sauce has thickened and the meatballs are cooked through, about 20 to 25 minutes.

Add the fish sauce, syrup, and snow peas, and cook for 2 minutes. Remove from the heat.

Divide into individual serving bowls, and garnish with basil. Serve with the rice and lime wedges alongside.

Kenyan-Style Coconut Chicken Curry (Kuku Paka) with Beatrice's Chapati

4 pounds bone-in chicken drumsticks

3 plum tomatoes, roughly chopped

1 large red onion, roughly chopped

2-inch piece fresh ginger, peeled

4 garlic cloves, peeled and smashed

3 serrano chilies, stemmed and seeded

¼ cup chopped fresh cilantro stems

2 teaspoons ground cumin

1½ teaspoons ground coriander

1 teaspoon ground turmeric

1 teaspoon garam masala

Sea salt and freshly ground black pepper

2 tablespoons coconut oil

2 cans (each 14 ounces) coconut milk

Juice of 1 lemon

For serving

½ cup chopped fresh cilantro

1 to 2 green chilies, sliced (if you like it extra spicy)

Chapati (page 207)

Rice (optional)

My beautiful friend Beatrice lives in Dzikunze, a remote village in the drought-ridden southeastern region of Kenya (second to my Canadian homeland, my absolute favorite place on planet earth). I've had the honor to visit Beatrice and her family several times, traveling there with my friends from World Vision Canada, and every time I leave inspired, challenged, and changed. Because of the persisting drought in the region, Beatrice's property often goes weeks (if not months) without substantial rain, making growing crops, feeding livestock, and, ultimately, putting food on the table, an incredible challenge. And through it all, in the face of adversity, she is one of the most generous, kind, gracious, and welcoming people I've ever had the pleasure to spend time with.

This recipe is inspired by a day spent cooking with Beatrice and her family. We prepared some of her family's favorite dishes—a slow-cooked chicken curry, packed with rich spices, fragrant ginger, cilantro, and coconut milk, and served alongside chapati, a golden crisp flatbread-style bread that may just be the most delicious bite you ever taste. Cooking this dish with Beatrice, her family, and friends is one of the greatest honors of my life. Thank you, Beatrice. You're an inspiration.

Score each piece of chicken 2 to 3 times with a sharp knife, slicing about ⅓ inch into the meat. Place the chicken in a large bowl.

In a food processor, place the tomatoes, onion, ginger, garlic, serrano chilies, cilantro stems, cumin, coriander, turmeric, garam masala, and a generous pinch each of salt and pepper, and pulse until a paste forms. Add one-third of the marinade to the chicken, and massage until the chicken is entirely coated. Cover with plastic wrap and refrigerate for at least 1 hour (although 4 hours is best). Cover the remaining paste with plastic wrap and refrigerate until it's time to cook.

Preheat a pellet grill or smoker to 180°F and get that smoke rolling.

Place the chicken directly on the grill grates and smoke for 30 minutes. Increase the grill temp to 350°F, and continue grilling the chicken until it reaches an internal temperature of 165°F, about 30 to 35 minutes. If you prefer to cook on a gas or charcoal grill, prepare the grill for indirect, medium–heat grilling (see Notes on Grilling, page 187). Start the chicken on the hotter side of the grill to brown the skin and render some of the fat, and then move to the cooler zone and cook over indirect heat until the internal temperature reaches 165°F, about 30 to 35 minutes.

recipe continues

While the chicken grills, heat the coconut oil in a large, high-sided skillet over medium heat. When the oil is hot, add the remaining marinade paste and cook, stirring often, until most of the moisture evaporates, about 15 to 20 minutes. Add the coconut milk, bring to a simmer, and let the sauce bubble away for 25 to 30 minutes, or until thickened. Season to taste with salt and pepper.

Add the grilled chicken to the sauce, and then bring to a simmer over medium heat to let all of those flavors mingle and spend a little quality time together. Squeeze in the lemon juice, and transfer to a large, deep serving platter. Top with the cilantro and green chilies (if you're feeling spicy), and serve with chapati and rice (if using) alongside.

BEATRICE'S CHAPATI

These unleavened flatbreads are quick and simple to make, but serve a valuable purpose—they're the perfect vehicle for sopping up the luscious curry sauce.

MAKES 4 LARGE CHAPATI

2 cups all-purpose flour, plus more for dusting

Sea salt

¾ cup lukewarm water

6 teaspoons grapeseed oil or other neutral oil, plus more for frying

Combine the flour and a couple pinches of salt in a large bowl and mix well. Add the water to the flour mixture and mix together thoroughly with a spoon until a sticky dough starts to form.

Turn the dough out onto a floured surface and get those arm muscles ready to rock. Using the palms of your hands, knead the dough until a very soft elastic dough ball forms, about 10 minutes. Cover the dough tightly with plastic wrap and let it rest on the counter for 20 minutes. (If you're planning ahead, the dough can be chilled in the fridge overnight at this step.)

Divide the dough into 4 equal portions, and shape each into a small ball. Working with one piece at a time on a floured surface, roll into an 8-inch round flatbread (think tortillas), about ⅛ inch thick. Spoon 1½ teaspoons of oil onto the surface of the flatbread, coating it entirely. Tightly roll the dough into itself (like a fruit roll-up), until you have a long snake-like tube of dough. Coil the rolled dough into a tight snail-shaped disk. Press and flatten the dough with the palm of your hand, and then roll out one final time on a floured surface into an 8-inch round flatbread. Repeat with the remaining balls of dough.

Heat 1 tablespoon of the grapeseed oil in a large cast-iron or heavy-bottomed skillet over medium heat. When the oil is hot, add 1 flatbread and fry for about 1 minute per side, or until golden brown and crispy. Repeat with the remaining chapatis.

These chapatis are the very best when served fresh and still warm, but will keep well for 1 to 2 days in an airtight container at room temperature; reheat in a dry skillet.

Mint and Aleppo Pepper Chicken Kebabs

3 tablespoons chicken stock, homemade (page 200) or store-bought

1½ tablespoons Aleppo pepper

2 teaspoons toasted coriander seeds, bashed in a mortar and pestle

1 teaspoon ground cumin

1 cup full-fat Greek yogurt

¼ cup extra-virgin olive oil

2 tablespoons red wine vinegar

2 tablespoons tomato paste

7 garlic cloves, minced

¼ cup finely chopped fresh mint, plus more for serving

Zest of 2 lemons

2½ pounds boneless skinless chicken thighs

Sea salt and freshly ground black pepper

For serving

Fresh flat-leaf parsley sprigs

1 lemon, cut into wedges

Pickled Red Onions (page 210)

Hummus (page 223) (optional)

Pita bread (optional)

Marinating chicken in creamy yogurt both tenderizes and flavors the chicken. I spike the yogurt with Aleppo pepper, which is smoky and slightly spicy; if you don't have any, you can substitute with sweet paprika with a good pinch of cayenne added in. This gorgeous yogurt marinade also has a righteous hit of garlic, as well as coriander, cumin, and fresh mint. My favorite way to serve these kebabs is with pickled red onions (page 210), a heaping helping of hummus (page 223), and a stack of warm pita bread.

In a large bowl, stir together the stock, Aleppo pepper, coriander, and cumin until a paste forms. Add the yogurt, olive oil, vinegar, and tomato paste, and whisk until well combined. Stir in the garlic, mint, and lemon zest, add the chicken thighs, and stir to coat the chicken with the yogurt mixture. Cover and refrigerate for at least 1 hour or up to 24 hours.

Prepare a grill for direct, medium-high heat grilling (see Notes on Grilling, page 187).

Using metal skewers, thread the chicken thighs onto the skewers, dividing equally. Season the chicken with salt and pepper, and transfer the skewers to the grill and grill, turning every couple of minutes, for 10 to 12 minutes, or until the chicken is golden, beautifully charred, and cooked through. Cut into a piece to test, or insert an instant-read thermometer into the thickest part of a piece of meat—it should register 165°F.

Transfer the skewers to a platter, garnish with the mint and parsley sprigs, and serve with the lemon wedges and pickled red onions alongside, and hummus (if using) and pita bread (if using).

PICKLED RED ONIONS

Pickling removes a lot of the bite from red onions, which can often be pretty fiery. It also turns them a beautiful pink color. More importantly, they're wildly delicious. I always like to have some on hand—they're great on burgers, tacos, salads, and sandwiches.

MAKES ABOUT 2 CUPS

1 large red onion, thinly sliced

1½ teaspoons fennel seeds

1½ teaspoons coriander seeds

1 teaspoon cumin seeds

1 teaspoon black peppercorns, bashed in a mortar and pestle

1 cup water

½ cup red wine vinegar

4 teaspoons honey

1½ teaspoons sea salt

Place the sliced onion in a pint jar.

Heat a skillet over medium heat, add the fennel, coriander, cumin seeds, and peppercorns, and toast, shaking the skillet, until fragrant, 2 minutes.

In a medium saucepan, combine the water, vinegar, honey, salt, and toasted spices, and bring to a boil. Pour the mixture over the onions, making sure that they're completely submerged in liquid. Cover and chill for at least 1 hour or up to 24 hours. Store the pickled onions in an airtight container in the refrigerator for up to 2 weeks.

Grilled Tequila-Chili Chicken Fajitas with Spiked Sour Cream

For the chicken

2 tablespoons extra-virgin olive oil, plus more for drizzling

¼ cup tequila

2 teaspoons chili powder

1 teaspoon smoked paprika

½ teaspoon ground cumin

¼ teaspoon cayenne pepper

Zest of 1 lime

Sea salt and freshly ground black pepper

2 pounds boneless, skinless chicken breasts

For the pico de gallo

1½ pounds ripe plum tomatoes

1 medium red onion, finely chopped

1 jalapeño pepper, finely chopped

½ cup fresh cilantro, chopped

Juice of 1 lime

Sea salt

For the sour cream

½ cup sour cream

1 tablespoon freshly squeezed lime juice

1 teaspoon chili powder

¼ teaspoon smoked paprika

Sea salt

For the peppers and onions

3 red or orange bell peppers, stemmed, seeded, and sliced

1 large red onion, cut into half-moons

Olive oil

Sea salt

Fajita night! Yes, please. When I was a kid, a local Moncton restaurant served show-stopping fajitas in fiery sizzling cast-iron pans and I've been hooked ever since. Quite possibly the perfect dish for feeding a hungry crowd, and reasonably healthy to boot! Let's be honest friends, chicken breasts can be bland, so I marinate the lean meat in a zesty combination of tequila, chili powder, smoked paprika, cumin, and cayenne, and then grill them quickly so they stay super juicy and tender. As always, a meat thermometer is essential in guaranteeing perfectly cooked-to-temp protein. Homemade pico de gallo, sour cream spiked with chili and lime, grilled vegetables, and flour tortillas round out these DIY fajitas into the perfect weeknight meal. Pile everything onto platters and in bowls and serve family-style.

Marinate the Chicken: In a resealable plastic bag, combine the olive oil, tequila, chili powder, paprika, cumin, cayenne, lime zest, salt, and pepper. Add the chicken breasts, seal the bag, and scrunch the bag so the chicken gets coated in the marinade. Refrigerate for at least 4 hours or up to 24 hours.

Preheat a grill for direct, medium-high heat grilling (see Notes on Grilling, page 187).

Make the Pico de Gallo: In a medium bowl, combine the tomatoes, onion, jalapeño, cilantro, and lime juice and stir to combine. Season to taste with salt.

Prepare the Sour Cream: In a small bowl, stir together the sour cream, lime juice, chili powder, and paprika, and season to taste with salt.

Grill the Chicken: When the grill is hot, remove the chicken from the marinade (discard the marinade) and place on the grill grate. Cook, turning occasionally, until an instant-read thermometer inserted in the thickest part of the breast reaches 165°F, about 10 to 12 minutes. Transfer to a plate and rest at least 5 minutes before carving.

Grill the Peppers and Onions: When the chicken has cooked for 6 minutes, drizzle the peppers and onion in a bit of olive oil and season with salt. Add the veggies to the grill alongside the chicken. Cook, carefully turning (so the vegetables don't slip through the grate) until tender and charred in spots, about 6 to 8 minutes. Transfer to a cutting board, cut into strips, and transfer to a platter.

Slice the chicken into thin, fajita-friendly strips. Pile on the platter alongside the grilled peppers and onions and serve with the pico de gallo, sour cream, avocado, jalapeños, radishes, cilantro, lime wedges, and tortillas.

ingredients continue

For serving

2 avocados, peeled, pitted, and cut into wedges

Your favorite toppings, including: sliced jalapeño pepper, thinly sliced radishes, fresh cilantro, and lime wedges

Warm Homemade Flour Tortillas (recipe at right)

HOMEMADE FLOUR TORTILLAS

Yes, flour tortillas are readily available, but homemade tortillas—pliant, warm from the pan, with leopard spots of char—are a cut above, and worth making yourself, at least from time to time. While traditionally these are made with lard, I've substituted vegetable oil here.

MAKES 10 TORTILLAS

2 cups all-purpose flour

1 teaspoon baking powder

1 teaspoon sea salt

1 tablespoon vegetable oil

¾ cup boiling water

In a medium bowl, combine the flour, baking powder, salt, and oil, and give everything a good mix. Add the water, and mix together with a fork until a dough ball starts to form. Turn out onto a floured surface, and then knead until a soft dough ball forms, 5 to 6 minutes. Wrap in plastic wrap and let rest at room temperature for 30 minutes.

Divide the dough into 10 equal portions and shape into small dough balls. Roll out each into a 6-inch round. Heat a 12-inch cast-iron skillet over medium heat, and cook the tortillas in batches of two for 1 to 2 minutes per side until golden and slightly charred. Keep warm in a clean kitchen towel while you prepare the rest.

Miso Marinated Grilled Chicken with Flavor-Bomb Pickles

For the chicken

1 cup white miso

1 cup mirin

½ cup sake

2 tablespoons soy sauce

2 tablespoons honey

2 teaspoons toasted sesame oil

10 skin-on, boneless chicken thighs (about 4 to 5 pounds)

For the pickles

1 English cucumber, thinly sliced

2 teaspoons kosher salt

⅓ cup rice vinegar

2 tablespoons sugar

2 tablespoons sesame seeds

For serving

Miso Butter Mushrooms with Garlic Bok Choy (optional)

Steamed jasmine rice (optional)

Toasted sesame seeds

Sliced green onions

Hot sauce

Miso, bless you, you marvelous mystery of umami-packed tastiness. This amazing ingredient is a simple and massively effective way to add an uppercut punch of flavor to chicken (and just about everything else under the sun). For this preparation, I prefer boneless, skin-on chicken thighs, which won't dry out on the grill. Because the marinade contains some sugar (in the form of mirin and honey), take care while grilling, turning as needed to prevent the sugar from burning. A sidekick of flavor-bomb pickles is a must, but I also love to serve this with Miso Butter Mushrooms with Garlic Bok Choy (page 64) and steamed rice.

Marinate the Chicken: In a medium bowl combine the miso, mirin, sake, soy, honey, and sesame oil in a bowl and mix well. Place the chicken in a resealable plastic bag and pour in the marinade. Refrigerate for at least 4 hours or up to 24 hours.

Make the Pickles: Toss the cucumbers and salt together in a medium bowl and let sit for 20 minutes. Rinse the salt off of the cucumbers, and place back in the bowl. Add the rice vinegar, sugar, and sesame seeds, mix well, cover, and refrigerate for up to 24 hours. Pickles will store beautifully in the fridge for up to one week, though they certainly won't last that long. Awesome.

Preheat a grill for direct, high-heat grilling (see Notes on Grilling, page 187).

Grill the Chicken: When the grill is hot, remove the chicken from the marinade (discard the marinade), and then place the chicken skin side down on the grill grate. Grill for 8 to 10 minutes, flip, and continue grilling for an additional 10 minutes, or until crispy on the outside and an instant-read thermometer inserted in the thickest part of the thigh reaches 165°F. Transfer to a cutting board and cut the chicken into strips.

Serve right away with the pickles, Miso Butter Mushrooms with Garlic Bok Choy (if using), and steamed rice (if using). Garnish with the sesame seeds, green onions, and hot sauce.

Smoky Lime Chicken with Grilled Jalapeño Hot Sauce

For the chicken

6 whole bone-in chicken legs
(about 3 to 4 pounds)

2 tablespoons extra-virgin olive oil

1 tablespoon smoked paprika

1 tablespoon coriander seeds,
bashed in a mortar and pestle

Zest of 1 lime

Sea salt and freshly ground
black pepper

For the hot sauce

6 medium jalapeño peppers

4 garlic cloves, peeled

6 sprigs fresh cilantro

2 green onions, cut into
1-inch pieces

1 tablespoon freshly squeezed
lime juice

2 tablespoons pure maple syrup

½ cup distilled white vinegar

1 teaspoon sea salt

For serving

Warm corn tortillas (optional)

Salsa (page 169) (optional)

Summer dinners are the best—simple, easy, and more often than not prepared on the grill, to maximize flavor and so you don't have to worry about heating up your kitchen. There are few things I love as much as grilling for my crew! This grilled smoky lime chicken, with a fiery grilled jalapeño sauce, is one of my absolute favorites. Serve it with a stack of warm corn tortillas, a homemade salsa (like my Avocado Pineapple Salsa, page 169), and a cerveza or two alongside.

Marinate the Chicken: Place the chicken legs in a large bowl, massage with the olive oil, paprika, coriander, and lime zest, and season with salt and pepper. Cover with plastic wrap and refrigerate for at least 4 hours or up to 24 hours.

Preheat a grill for direct, medium-high heat grilling (see Notes on Grilling, page 187).

Make the Hot Sauce: When the grill is hot, place the jalapeños directly on the grill grates and cook until beautifully charred all over, 25 to 30 minutes.

Remove the stems from the jalapeños, place in a blender, and add the garlic, cilantro, green onions, lime juice, syrup, vinegar, and salt. Blend until smooth. Taste and adjust the seasoning as necessary. This can be made in advance and stored in an airtight container in the refrigerator for up to 2 weeks (I almost always have a bottle or two hanging out in there). Leftover sauce can be used on tacos, burgers, scrambled eggs, or nachos—anywhere you'd like a little heat.

Grill the Chicken: Place the chicken directly on the grill grates, skin side down (skin side up if you're using a pellet grill), and cook for 40 to 45 minutes, flipping every 10 minutes or so (no need to flip if using a pellet grill) or until perfectly golden, smoke-kissed, and an instant-read thermometer inserted into the thickest part of the chicken reaches 165°F. Rest at least 10 minutes before serving with the hot sauce alongside. Serve with corn tortillas and salsa alongside, if using.

Dijon and Tarragon Braised Chicken and Potatoes

8 bone-in, skin-on chicken thighs (about 3 pounds)

Sea salt and freshly ground black pepper

2 tablespoons extra-virgin olive oil

2 tablespoons unsalted butter

1 large Vidalia onion, diced

1½ tablespoons chopped fresh thyme

4 garlic cloves, minced

1 cup dry white wine

1½ cups chicken stock, homemade (page 200) or store-bought

¼ cup Dijon mustard

2 tablespoons honey

Zest of 1 lemon

1½ tablespoons minced fresh tarragon

2 pounds baby new potatoes

¼ cup chopped fresh flat-leaf parsley

Inspired by a lunchtime chicken dish I had at a quaint Parisian bistro, this simple braise has a velvety pan sauce flavored with white wine, Dijon mustard, and fresh thyme and tarragon, which contribute to herbaceous freshness. I cook baby new potatoes in the braising liquid alongside the chicken, making this an elegant one-pan dinner. A simple salad and some crusty bread alongside for mopping up the luscious sauce, and a glass or two of crisp white wine, are all that is needed to complete this meal.

Preheat the oven to 375°F.

Season the chicken all over with salt and pepper. Heat the olive oil in a large, high-sided, oven-safe skillet over medium heat. When the oil is hot, add the chicken, skin side down, and cook until the skin is golden and crispy, about 4 to 5 minutes. With tongs, transfer the chicken to a rimmed plate or baking sheet, leaving the excess oil in the skillet.

Add the butter to the skillet. When the butter is melted, add the onion and thyme, season with a pinch of salt, and cook until softened and translucent, about 6 to 8 minutes. Add the garlic, cook for 45 seconds, and then pour in the wine and stock. Add the mustard, honey, lemon zest, and tarragon, season with a few pinches of salt and pepper, and stir to combine. Add the potatoes and return the chicken (skin side up) to the skillet and bring to a boil.

Transfer the skillet to the oven and cook uncovered, until an instant-read thermometer inserted into the thickest part of a chicken thigh reaches 165°F and the potatoes are fork-tender, 25 to 30 minutes. Garnish with the parsley and serve.

Turkey Roulade with Bourbon, Pancetta, Cranberry, and Leeks

For the brine

1 gallon water

1 cup sea salt

1 cup brown sugar

1 cup bourbon

3 clementines, halved

2 rosemary sprigs

For the roulade

1 turkey breast (5 to 6 pounds), deboned, with skin on

2 tablespoons unsalted butter

7 ounces chopped pancetta

2 leeks, white and light green parts only, thinly sliced

1 large fennel bulb, thinly sliced

1 tablespoon minced fresh sage

1 tablespoon chopped fresh thyme

1 tablespoon chopped fresh rosemary, plus 2 rosemary sprigs

Sea salt

2 garlic cloves, minced

1½ cups bourbon, divided

½ cup cranberries

Zest of 1 clementine

Juice of 2 clementines

¾ cup panko breadcrumbs

Freshly ground black pepper

2 tablespoons extra-virgin olive oil

1½ cups turkey stock (or chicken stock)

2 clementines, halved

Everyone needs that recipe or two in their rolodex of recipes that are tailor-made to impress. Big, bold, family-friendly, and perfect for celebrating at the communal table. Though a whole roasted turkey may be the traditional centerpiece of a Thanksgiving or Friendsgiving feast, this roulade—made with a deboned whole turkey breast, filled with a breadcrumb stuffing flavored with cranberries and clementines—is a worthy (and arguably more delicious) alternative. The boneless roulade is easy to cut into neat slices, and leftovers can be easily carved for superlative (and necessary) day-after turkey sandwiches. The garlicky mashed potatoes on page 67 are a perfect accompaniment.

Make the Brine: Combine the water, salt, and sugar in the largest stockpot you have and heat over medium-low heat, stirring, just until the sugar and salt have dissolved. Pour in the bourbon, add the clementines and rosemary, and let cool to room temperature.

Prepare the Roulade: Place the turkey breast skin side down on a work surface. Starting with the narrowest end of the meat and holding the blade of the knife parallel to your work surface, make a horizontal cut about halfway through the thickness of the meat. Continue cutting with your blade parallel to the work surface, creating two equally thick layers of turkey. Make sure not to cut all the way through the meat, stopping when there is still about ¾ inch of meat remaining. You should now be able to open the turkey to lay flat, like an open book, to make a uniformly thick, large piece of meat.

Place a piece of plastic wrap over the breast, and pound with a meat mallet into an even rectangle, about ¼ inch thick. Place the turkey breast into the brine. Refrigerate for at least 1 hour or up to 4 hours (no longer, though, or the meat will become too salty).

Heat a large cast-iron or oven-safe high-sided skillet over medium heat. Add the butter, and when the butter has melted add the pancetta and fry, stirring frequently, until crispy and golden. With a slotted spoon, transfer the pancetta to a plate, leaving behind the fat in the skillet. Add the leeks, fennel, sage, thyme, and chopped rosemary, season with a pinch of salt, and cook, stirring occasionally, until softened, about 6 to 8 minutes. Stir in the garlic, pour in ½ cup of the bourbon, and add the cranberries, clementine zest, and clementine juice. Bring to a simmer, remove from the heat, and stir in the panko breadcrumbs. Season with salt and pepper to taste and mix well. Transfer to a bowl, and let the stuffing cool for a few minutes. Wipe out the skillet (you'll be using it again).

recipe continues

Remove the turkey breast from the brine and pat dry with paper towel. Transfer to a cutting board, skin side down. Spread the stuffing mixture all over the flesh side of the turkey breast, leaving a 1-inch border. Tightly roll the turkey breast up like a jelly roll, and then tie the roulade at 1-inch intervals. Drizzle the roulade with the olive oil and season with an extra pinch of salt and pepper.

Preheat the cast-iron skillet over medium-high heat. When the skillet is hot, carefully place the turkey roulade into the skillet and cook, turning as needed, until the skin is starting to crisp and turn golden brown, 8 to 10 minutes. Pour in the remaining 1 cup of the bourbon, stock, halved clementines, and rosemary sprigs. Transfer to the oven and roast for about 1½ to 2 hours, or until the turkey reaches an internal temperature of 160°F. (The internal temperature of your roulade will increase as it rests. As always with protein, we're cooking to temperature, not time. Your trusty meat thermometer is essential here.)

Transfer the roulade to a cutting board, tent with foil, rest for at least 20 minutes, and then carve into ½-inch slices. Spoon some of the pan juices over the sliced meat (if making a gravy, save those pan juices for it—pro tip) and serve with all your favorite side dishes.

Cooking Note: *I like to spike the stuffing and the pan sauce with some bourbon, but if you prefer, you can substitute additional turkey or chicken stock.*

Spiced Lamb Meatballs with Hummus and Tomato-Cucumber Salad

For the hummus

1 pound dry chickpeas

1½ teaspoons baking soda

1 large head garlic

¼ cup extra-virgin olive oil, plus more for drizzling

1½ teaspoons sea salt, plus pinch more

Freshly ground black pepper

Juice of ½ lemon

⅓ cup tahini

¼ cup water

¼ teaspoon ground cumin

¼ teaspoon smoked paprika

For the meatballs

1½ pounds ground lamb

½ cup unseasoned dry breadcrumbs

2 tablespoons chopped mint

2 tablespoons chopped fresh cilantro

1 large egg

2 garlic cloves, minced

1 teaspoon smoked paprika

Zest of 1 lemon

Sea salt and freshly ground black pepper

2 tablespoons extra-virgin olive oil

Inspired by my time in sun-soaked Dubai, Cairo, and the Mediterranean, this plate of happiness is everything I love in a dish. Across the region it's common to find generous plates of warm, freshly made hummus topped with spiced meat, often with a simple tomato and cucumber salad served alongside. This is my version, with tender lamb meatballs, fluffy roasted garlic hummus, and a one-bowl salad that adds freshness and crunch. Though it seems like a reasonable shortcut to substitute prepared hummus, please don't—the difference between creamy, freshly made hummus and store-bought is night and day, and well worth the extra effort.

Make the Hummus: Place the uncooked chickpeas and baking soda in a large bowl and cover with 2 inches of water. Cover with plastic wrap and chill in the fridge overnight. The next day, drain and rinse your chickpeas. Transfer to a large stockpot and cover with 2 inches of water. Bring to a boil over high heat, reduce to a simmer, and cook for 45 minutes to 1 hour, until fork-tender (but not mushy).

Slice about ¼ inch off the top of the garlic bulb, exposing the cloves but leaving the root intact. Drizzle the exposed cloves with olive oil, season with a pinch of salt and pepper, and wrap tightly in tinfoil. Roast for 30 to 35 minutes, until the cloves are very soft. Squeeze the garlic cloves onto a board, and mash them into a paste.

In the base of the food processor, combine the chickpeas, roasted garlic paste, and 1½ teaspoons of salt and pulse for 30 seconds, scraping the sides of the processor down if necessary. Add the lemon juice, tahini, water, cumin, and paprika, and pulse for 30 more seconds, until combined. With the food processor running, slowly drizzle in the ¼ cup of olive oil and continue processing until the hummus is smooth and fluffy, about 3 minutes. If you're planning to serve right away, transfer to a bowl. If you're making ahead, transfer to a lidded container and refrigerate for up to 4 days, until ready to serve. Let come to room temperature before serving. If the hummus is stiff, whisk in some warm water. Set aside.

Make the Meatballs: Combine the lamb, breadcrumbs, mint, cilantro, egg, garlic, paprika, lemon zest, and salt and pepper in a large bowl. Mix well, and then shape into small, golf ball–sized meatballs. Heat the olive oil in a large oven-safe skillet over medium heat. When the oil is hot, add the meatballs and cook, turning, until browned on all sides, about 6 minutes. Transfer the skillet to the oven and bake until the meatballs are cooked through (cut one to test—it should be a bit pink right in the center), about 10 minutes.

ingredients and recipe continue

223

For the salad

2 large plum tomatoes, cored and diced

½ English cucumber, diced

½ red onion, diced

Juice of ½ lemon

1 tablespoon extra-virgin olive oil

Sea salt and freshly ground black pepper

For serving

½ cup Greek yogurt

¼ cup crumbled feta cheese

2 tablespoons roasted pine nuts

2 tablespoons pomegranate arils

Handful fresh mint

Handful fresh cilantro

Pita bread

Make the Salad: In a medium bowl combine the tomatoes, cucumber, onion, lemon, and olive oil, and season to taste with salt and pepper. Toss to mix and set aside.

To serve, spoon about ¼ cup of hummus onto each serving plate, and top with a few of the meatballs. Divide the salad onto each plate, and dollop on the yogurt, dividing evenly. Sprinkle over the feta cheese, pine nuts, and pomegranate arils, and garnish with the mint and cilantro. Serve with the pita bread alongside.

Lamb Shawarma with Labneh and Pine Nuts

1 tablespoon cumin seeds

1 teaspoon coriander seeds

1 teaspoon fennel seeds

1 teaspoon ground allspice

¼ teaspoon ground turmeric

¼ teaspoon cinnamon

¼ teaspoon ground ginger

¼ teaspoon cayenne pepper

½ cup extra-virgin olive oil

1 large onion, roughly chopped

6 garlic cloves

Juice of 1 lemon

1½ teaspoons sea salt, plus more for serving

½ teaspoon freshly ground black pepper

1 bone-in lamb shoulder (3½ pounds)

4½ cups chicken stock, homemade (page 200) or store-bought

1 lemon, cut into wedges

3 cups labneh

¼ cup roasted pine nuts

1 cup pickled red onions (page 210)

1 to 2 very finely chopped bird's eye or Thai chilies (optional)

¼ cup fresh mint

6 to 8 warm pita breads, for serving

Street food, in my humble opinion, is the best food. In many parts of the world where I've been fortunate enough to visit, lamb shawarma reigns supreme as the street food of choice. The golden spit-roasted meat is carved to order, piled on warm flatbread with hot sauce and fresh herbs, and wrapped into a convenient handheld parcel. Inspired by those late-night grab-and-go meals, I've created a home cook–friendly version. It's not fast food, but it's mostly hands-off slow cooking time, and the spice-crusted pieces of fork-tender lamb are absolutely worth waiting for. Serve this alongside warm pita, a crisp summery salad, and your favorite hot sauce.

Combine the cumin, coriander, and fennel seeds in a dry skillet and toast over medium-low heat until fragrant, about 3 to 4 minutes. Cool for a few minutes, and then grind in a mortar and pestle (or spice grinder).

In a food processor, combine the toasted ground spices, allspice, turmeric, cinnamon, ginger, cayenne, olive oil, onion, garlic, lemon juice, salt, and pepper and pulse until a paste starts to form. Rub all over the lamb, coating completely, transfer to a baking dish, and cover with plastic wrap. Marinate in the fridge for at least 12 hours, or for up to 24 hours.

Preheat the oven (or grill) to 450°F. Place the lamb in a shallow roasting pan and roast for 20 to 25 minutes, until a beautifully golden color starts to form all over the lamb.

Reduce the heat to 350°F, and pour the stock into the roasting pan. Add the lemon wedges, cover the pan with foil, and cook for about 4 hours, basting the lamb every hour or so, until the meat falls off the bone and reaches about 195°F on an instant-read thermometer.

Using two forks, shred the lamb into bite-size pieces. Discard the bone. Reserve the meat and pan juices.

Grab a large serving tray. Spoon the labneh in an even layer over the tray, and top with the shredded lamb. Spoon over some of those beautiful pan juices and sprinkle with salt. Top with the pine nuts, pickled red onions, chilies (if using), and mint. Serve with warm pita alongside.

My Favorite Swedish Meatballs

⅓ cup panko breadcrumbs

½ cup whole milk

1 large egg

2 tablespoons chopped fresh flat-leaf parsley

2 garlic cloves, minced

¼ teaspoon ground allspice

¼ teaspoon nutmeg

½ medium yellow onion, finely chopped

1 pound quality ground beef (80/20)

½ pound quality ground pork

½ teaspoon sea salt, plus more to taste

¼ teaspoon freshly ground black pepper, plus more to taste

5 tablespoons unsalted butter, divided

1 tablespoon extra-virgin olive oil

¼ cup all-purpose flour

2 cups beef broth, warmed

1 cup heavy (35%) cream, warmed

1 tablespoon Worcestershire sauce

1 teaspoon Dijon mustard

I first visited Sweden during midsummer, the celebration of the summer solstice, the longest day of the year, and one of the most celebrated holidays for Swedes. Golden hour seems to last forever, creating an almost cinematic glow to evenings spent dining on patios or sharing a drink with new friends. After I landed from my long transatlantic voyage, the first thing I did was go to a locally recommended restaurant and order, of course, meatballs. Most people only know Swedish meatballs from the ones they sell at IKEA. But it's a breeze to make a scratch-made version that's much, much better. The meatballs are bound with a panade, a combination of breadcrumbs and milk that adds moisture and makes the meatballs exceptionally tender. Traditionally the meatballs are served with mashed potatoes (page 67), lingonberry jam, and pickled cucumbers, which is an unbeatable Scandinavian combination, though you could also serve the meatballs with buttered egg noodles or your favorite greens, like crisp steamed green beans.

In a large bowl, combine the breadcrumbs, milk, egg, parsley, garlic, allspice, and nutmeg, and mix well. Let sit for about 10 minutes, until the breadcrumbs have absorbed the milk. Add the onion, beef, pork, salt, and pepper, and mix gently but thoroughly until well combined. Shape into 16 to 18 large meatballs (if you prefer smaller meatballs, that's cool—just roll them smaller).

To a large skillet over medium heat, add 2 tablespoons of the butter and the olive oil. When the butter has melted, add the meatballs and cook, turning, until browned on all sides and cooked through, about 6 minutes. Using a slotted spoon, transfer the meatballs to a plate and set aside.

With the skillet still over medium heat, whisk in the remaining 3 tablespoons of the butter and the flour, and cook, whisking, until the mixture is bubbling and beginning to turn a light tan color. In a slow and steady stream, whisk in the broth, followed by the cream. Whisk in the Worcestershire and mustard. Season to taste with salt and pepper, and then bring the sauce to a simmer. Cook until thickened, about 4 to 5 minutes. Return the meatballs to the skillet and cook for another 1 to 2 minutes, until warmed through.

Hoisin Pork Meatballs

1½ pounds quality ground pork

1 tablespoon mayonnaise, homemade (page 118) or store-bought

3 garlic cloves, minced

1-inch piece fresh ginger, peeled and minced

1 teaspoon curry powder

2 tablespoons chopped fresh cilantro

Zest of 1 lime

Sea salt

½ cup chicken stock, homemade (page 200) or store-bought

½ cup hoisin sauce

¼ cup soy sauce

1 tablespoon packed brown sugar

1 tablespoon grapeseed or other neutral oil

2 teaspoons toasted sesame seeds

2 green onions, thinly sliced

These little bundles of joy are irresistible. Hoisin and pork are the best of friends, and this weeknight recipe is guaranteed to quickly become a family favorite. Flavored with garlic, ginger, and curry, they're browned until golden and then finished in a sticky-sweet glaze made from hoisin sauce, soy sauce, and a bit of brown sugar. Heads up! The addition of mayonnaise to the meatballs may seem odd, but it's a game-changer, and helps to bind the meatballs and keep them extra juicy. I love to serve these meatballs with fluffy steamed jasmine rice and some garlicky sautéed bok choy or kale, or tossed with Chinese egg noodles. If you're feeling spicy (like I often am), a spoonful of chili crunch is the ultimate condiment.

In a medium bowl, combine the pork, mayonnaise, garlic, ginger, curry, cilantro, and lime zest, season with a good pinch of salt, and mix well. Roll the mixture into small golf ball–sized meatballs.

In a medium bowl, whisk together the chicken stock, hoisin, soy sauce, and brown sugar.

Heat the grapeseed oil in a medium skillet over medium heat. When the oil is hot, and working in batches as necessary, add the meatballs and cook, turning, until browned on all sides, about 3 to 4 minutes. Add the sauce to the meatballs and bring to a simmer. Simmer for about 5 to 6 minutes, until the sauce is lightly thickened and glorious, and the meatballs are cooked through. Remove from the heat, add the sesame seeds and green onions, and toss to coat.

Summertime Sheet-Pan Sausage Supper

½ medium red onion, sliced

1 green zucchini, cut into ½-inch rounds

1 yellow summer squash, cut into ½-inch rounds

1 red bell pepper, stemmed, seeded, and sliced

1 pound cherry tomatoes

4 garlic cloves, minced

1 tablespoon minced fresh rosemary

Sea salt and freshly ground black pepper

⅓ cup extra-virgin olive oil

1 pound sweet or hot Italian sausages

1 lemon, halved

1 batch Herbed Vinaigrette (page 249)

1½ cups baby arugula

¼ cup minced basil

Like the vegetarian sheet-pan supper on page 130, this weeknight friendly meaty version is a simple method for preparing a complete meal using a single dish. I love the way the flavorful fat from the sausages gently bastes the vegetables as they cook. You can use sweet or hot Italian sausages for this recipe, or another variety, if you prefer—but avoid pre-cooked sausages, which will become over-cooked before the vegetables are done. Though this dish requires nothing extra, it is wonderful with creamy polenta (page 175), crispy potato wedges, or a big summer salad alongside.

Preheat the oven (or grill) to 400°F.

On a large, rimmed baking sheet combine the onion, zucchini, squash, bell pepper, tomatoes, garlic, and rosemary. Season with salt and pepper, drizzle over the olive oil, and toss to mix.

Nestle the sausage links and lemon halves among the vegetables, transfer to the oven, and bake, flipping everything halfway through, until the vegetables are softened and beginning to caramelize and the sausages are browned and cooked through, 25 to 30 minutes or reaching 160°F using a meat thermometer.

Spoon the vinaigrette over the hot sausages and vegetables. Top with arugula and basil, hit with an extra few cracks of black pepper, and serve.

Spicy Lentil and Chorizo Soup with Fried Tortilla Strips

1 tablespoon extra-virgin olive oil

6 ounces pork chorizo, casings removed

2 jalapeño peppers, one minced, one thinly sliced, for garnish

¼ cup minced fresh cilantro stems

1 large yellow onion, finely chopped

2 medium carrots, peeled and finely chopped

Sea salt

1 tablespoon tomato paste

3 garlic cloves, minced

2 cups red lentils, rinsed

1 can (14 ounces) crushed tomatoes

6½ cups chicken stock, homemade (page 200) or store-bought

1 teaspoon smoked paprika

Grapeseed oil or other neutral oil, for frying

2 cups corn tortillas, cut into thin strips

¼ cup Mexican-style crema or full-fat sour cream

½ cup queso fresco

¼ cup chopped fresh cilantro, for garnish

Lime wedges, for serving

On a blustery cold winter night, this soup—hearty, a little spicy, and fully loaded with flavor-packed toppings—is one of my go-to recipes. The addition of chorizo in the soup goes a long way in flavoring the lentils, bolstered by jalapeños and smoked paprika. And I especially like red lentils, which cook quickly, meaning this soup is perfect for a speedy weeknight supper. I don't find the task of frying tortilla strips too onerous, but if you do, you can top your soup with a handful of crushed tortilla chips (an easy hack). And if you like a bit of tanginess, garnish the soup with pickled jalapeños instead of fresh.

Heat the olive oil in a large stockpot over medium heat until the oil is shimmering. Carefully add the chorizo and cook, breaking up with a wooden spoon, until browned. Remove the chorizo with a slotted spoon, leaving the oil in the pot, and set aside.

Add the minced jalapeño, cilantro stems, onion, and carrot, season with salt, and cook until softened, about 7 to 8 minutes. Stir in the tomato paste and garlic, and cook for 2 minutes. Stir in the lentils and cook, stirring, for 1 minute. Return the chorizo to the pot and pour in the tomatoes, stock, and paprika. Season with salt and bring the soup to a simmer over medium heat. Cook, stirring every few minutes, until the soup is creamy and thickened and the lentils are tender, about 35 to 40 minutes. Taste and adjust the seasoning as necessary.

While the soup is simmering, prepare the fried tortilla garnish. Line a plate with paper towels and set nearby. In a saucepan, pour the grapeseed oil to a depth of 2 inches. Heat over medium heat until the oil reaches 350°F on a deep-frying thermometer. When hot, and working in batches as necessary, fry the tortillas until crispy and golden brown, 2 to 3 minutes. With a slotted spoon, transfer to the prepared plate and season with salt.

Divide your soup among individual serving bowls. Top with crispy tortillas and drizzle over the crema. Crumble the queso fresco on top of each bowl, and garnish with sliced jalapeños and cilantro. Serve immediately, with lime wedges alongside.

Change-Your-Life-Good Smoked Pulled Pork Sandwiches

For the pork

1 tablespoon whole coriander seeds

1 tablespoon lemon zest

1 tablespoon finely ground espresso

1 tablespoon brown sugar

1 tablespoon sea salt

1½ teaspoons freshly ground black pepper

1½ teaspoons smoked paprika

1½ teaspoons chili powder

One bone-in pork butt, about 6 to 9 pounds

For the coleslaw

5 cups shredded red cabbage

2 carrots, peeled and grated

1 large apple, grated

¼ cup minced fresh flat-leaf parsley

1 cup mayonnaise

1 tablespoon whole-grain mustard

1 tablespoon apple cider vinegar

2 teaspoons pure maple syrup

2 tablespoons freshly squeezed lemon juice

½ teaspoon celery seed

Sea salt and freshly ground black pepper

For serving

12 to 14 brioche buns, toasted

2 cups sliced bread and butter pickles

Your favorite barbecue sauce

Your favorite hot sauce

When I moved to Nashville, I couldn't cook (anything). I loved food and had the good fortune to try exciting dishes as I traveled with my band all over creation, but proper barbecue was a mystery to this Maritimer. I vividly remember gathering my pennies, visiting Jack's BBQ on Broadway, and ordering a classic pulled pork meat and three. From that first bite, I was done for. The depth of flavor, the perfect balance of smoky and sweet notes, the texture, and the accessible yet elevated nature of that dish was simply mind blowing. And even after all these years, all of the travel, and all of the incredible ingredients that I've been blessed to work with, I always come back to barbecue.

Several times every summer, we gather a big crew and I slow-cook a giant pork butt until it's pull-apart tender, make a big bowl of cabbage slaw, and set a mountain of buns alongside so everyone can make their own sandwich. The simple yet delicious spice rub I use on the pork is fantastic on all sorts of other meats, too—try it on steak, grilled chicken pieces, or pork chops.

Prepare the Pork: Combine the coriander seeds, lemon zest, espresso, brown sugar, salt, pepper, paprika, and chili powder in a small bowl and mix well. Trim any excess fat from the pork butt. Generously coat every nook and cranny of the pork butt with the rub, using all of it, and refrigerate for at least 8 hours or up to 24 hours.

Preheat a grill or smoker to 250°F and get that smoke rolling.

Place the pork butt directly on the grill grate and insert a meat probe. Cook until the internal temperature reads 160°F, about 3 to 4 hours. Remove and wrap the pork tightly in a double layer of heavy-duty aluminum foil. Return the meat to the grill, reinsert the meat probe, and cook until the pork reaches an internal temperature of 204°F, about 3 to 4 hours longer, depending on the size of the pork butt.

Remove from the grill and let rest, still wrapped in the foil, for 45 minutes. Patience is required here, but well worth the wait.

Make the Coleslaw: In a large bowl combine the cabbage, carrot, apple, and parsley. In a second bowl, combine the mayo, mustard, vinegar, syrup, lemon juice, and celery seed, and season with salt and pepper to taste. Pour the dressing over the cabbage mixture and mix until well combined. Season to taste with additional salt and pepper.

After the pork has rested, remove from the foil. Carefully pour off any juices that have accumulated in the foil and reserve. Remove and discard any excess fat from the exterior of the meat. Using two forks, shred the meat— remove and discard the bone and any intramuscular fat.

Transfer the pork to a large serving platter, pour over the reserved juices, and sprinkle with salt. Serve with the toasted buns, coleslaw, pickles, barbecue sauce, and hot sauce.

Orange and Fennel Braised Pork Ragù

2 tablespoons extra-virgin olive oil

1 tablespoon unsalted butter

One boneless pork shoulder (4 pounds), tied

Sea salt and freshly ground black pepper

4 strips bacon, chopped

1 large white onion, diced

2 large carrots, peeled and diced

2 celery stalks, diced

1 tablespoon chopped fresh basil stems

1 tablespoon fennel seeds

4 garlic cloves, minced

1 tablespoon tomato paste

1 tablespoon fresh thyme, chopped

2 cups dry white wine

4 cups chicken stock, homemade (page 200) or store-bought

⅓ cup heavy (35%) cream

Zest of 1 orange

1 tablespoon Dijon mustard

⅓ cup minced fresh flat-leaf parsley

⅓ cup minced fresh basil

½ cup finely grated Parmesan cheese

I created this recipe while working alongside Justin Haber, a Maltese goalkeeper turned restaurateur, at his idyllically located restaurant Haber 16, just a stone's throw from the Marsaxlokk fish market, on the steps of the mighty Mediterranean. Maltese cuisine is incredibly unique and wonderfully diverse, having roots in Italian, Sicilian, Arabic, and North African cuisine, to mention but a few. I created this dish, subbing the locally celebrated rabbit for a more easily accessed pork shoulder.

In my home cook–friendly version, the pork shoulder is cooked in an aromatic braising liquid until it's fall-apart tender, then shredded, and returned to the pot. The juices are enriched with heavy cream, which makes the ragù especially luscious. My favorite bit—the combination of orange and pork. I add a generous amount of zest at the end of cooking, which gives the braise incredible fragrance and citrusy brightness, paying homage to the use of orange in Maltese cuisine. Serve this with polenta or tossed with pasta. As with all braises, this improves upon sitting, so don't hesitate to make it ahead.

Preheat the oven (or grill) to 325°F.

In a large Dutch oven or high-sided oven-safe pot over medium-high heat, combine the olive oil and butter. Season the pork shoulder all over with salt and pepper. When the butter has melted, add the pork to the pot and brown on all sides, about 6 to 8 minutes. With tongs, transfer to a rimmed plate or baking sheet.

Add the bacon, onion, carrot, celery, basil stems, and fennel seeds to the pot, and cook, stirring, until the vegetables are softened, 8 to 10 minutes. Add the garlic, tomato paste, and thyme, and cook for 2 minutes, stirring often. Pour in the wine and stock, and season with a pinch of salt and pepper. Return the pork shoulder to the pot, cover, and transfer to the oven. Braise for 2 hours, and then remove the cover and continue cooking an additional 1 to 2 hours, until the meat shreds easily. Check the pot occasionally; if the braising liquid gets too low, add a little chicken stock to the pot—the liquid should come one-third of the way up the pork while cooking. If the braising liquid is bubbling too vigorously, reduce the oven temperature to 300°F.

Remove the pork from the pot and transfer to a cutting board. Shred the meat using two forks. Meanwhile, skim and discard the fat from the surface of the braising liquid. Add the cream and bring to a simmer over medium heat. Let the sauce simmer and bubble away for about 6 to 8 minutes, or until reduced and lightly thickened.

Return the shredded meat to the pot. Stir in the orange zest, mustard, parsley, and basil. Finally, stir in the Parmesan and season with a few cracks of pepper.

Lamb Kofta Burgers

Burger night = best night. While I adore traditional beef burgers, these spiced lamb burgers are a wonderful spin on a beloved classic, and perfect for mixing up that same-old go-to burger recipe. I like to serve them feast-style with an array of toppings so everyone can build and customize their own. You can pan-fry the burgers, sure, but I think they're best grilled. A touch of char and smoke complements the meat wonderfully, and you can grill vegetables—think red bell peppers, eggplant, and zucchini—to serve alongside the burgers. I like to tuck the burgers into split pita bread, but you can also use traditional buns.

Preheat a grill for direct, high-heat grilling (see Notes on Grilling, page 187).

In a large bowl, mix together the lamb, garlic, onion, parsley, mint, coriander, paprika, cumin, and cayenne. Season generously with salt and pepper, and shape the mixture into 6 burger patties.

In a large bowl, toss the eggplant and red pepper with a glug of olive oil, and season with salt and pepper. Transfer to the grill, placing directly on the grill grates, and cook until slightly charred and slightly crispy, 8 to 10 minutes. Remove and set aside.

Add the lamb burgers to the grill and cook for 4 to 5 minutes per side for medium-cooked burgers (cook longer if you prefer your burgers a little more well done).

Season the cucumber, spinach, and tomato with salt and pepper. Arrange on a platter alongside the pickled red onions, feta, basil, tzatziki, and pita breads.

Serve the burgers with the platter of toppings alongside, and let everyone build and customize their own burger.

For the burgers and vegetables

1½ pounds ground lamb

4 garlic cloves, minced

1 medium onion, finely minced

1 tablespoon chopped fresh flat-leaf parsley

1 tablespoon chopped fresh mint

1½ teaspoons ground coriander

1½ teaspoons smoked paprika

1 teaspoon ground cumin

¼ teaspoon cayenne pepper

Sea salt and freshly ground black pepper

1 large eggplant, cut into ½-inch rounds

1 red bell pepper, julienned

Extra-virgin olive oil

For serving

1 cucumber, sliced, for topping

2 cups baby spinach, for topping

1 tomato, thinly sliced, for topping

Sea salt and freshly ground black pepper

¼ cup pickled red onions (page 210)

¼ cup crumbled feta cheese

¼ cup fresh basil

½ cup tzatziki

6 warm pita breads

Beef and Chorizo Burgers with Caramelized Onions

For the onions

2 tablespoons unsalted butter

3 large yellow onions, sliced

1 tablespoon chopped fresh thyme

Sea salt

2 garlic cloves, minced

For the burgers

1¼ pounds ground beef (80/20)

½ pound fresh chorizo sausage, removed from casings

2 tablespoons tomato paste

2 garlic cloves, minced

2 tablespoons finely chopped fresh basil

¼ cup finely grated Parmesan cheese

1 large egg

2 tablespoons unseasoned dry breadcrumbs

Sea salt and freshly ground black pepper

2 tablespoons grapeseed oil or other neutral oil

2 tablespoons unsalted butter

4 garlic cloves, skin on and gently crushed

2 sprigs fresh rosemary

¼ cup crumbled gorgonzola cheese, for topping

4 brioche burger buns, toasted

⅓ cup Secret-Weapon Burger Sauce (page 244)

½ cup baby arugula, for topping

I'm always down for a classic stacked-up burger with melty cheese and iceberg lettuce, but sometimes you need to pull out all the stops, and this recipe is the result. It's unique, wonderfully flavorful, and dressed to impress. I love the marriage of ground beef and chorizo, and I further jack up the flavor of the patties to 10,000% with the addition of Parmesan, garlic, and fragrant fresh basil. These burgers are topped with golden caramelized onions, rich gorgonzola cheese, and peppery arugula. Also! I tend to make extra caramelized onions whenever called for in recipes (which I highly recommend), as they're just about the perfect topping on burgers, in pasta, on grilled cheese sandwiches, blended with sour cream for a quick dip—the possibilities are endless.

Prepare the Onions: In a medium saucepan over medium-low heat, melt the butter. When the butter has melted, add the onions and thyme, season with a pinch of salt, and cook, stirring often, until golden and caramelized, 40 to 45 minutes. Add the garlic and cook, stirring, until fragrant, 1 minute more. Remove from the heat. Season again to taste and set aside.

Make the Burgers: In a large bowl combine the beef, chorizo, tomato paste, garlic, basil, Parmesan, egg, and breadcrumbs, and season generously with salt and pepper. Divide the mixture and shape into 4 burger patties, slightly larger than the width of your burger buns. Press a thumbprint into the center of each burger patty—this will prevent them from shrinking and doming up as they cook. Season both sides of each patty with salt and pepper.

Heat the grapeseed oil in a 12-inch cast-iron skillet over medium heat. When the oil is hot, add the burger patties and cook for 4 minutes. Flip the patties, and add the butter, garlic cloves, and rosemary to the skillet. When the butter has melted, continually baste the burgers with butter until cooked through, about 4 minutes. Top with gorgonzola cheese, dividing evenly, and remove the burger patties from the skillet.

Set each patty on a toasted bun spread with a heaping tablespoon of Burger Sauce. Top with the caramelized onions and arugula, dividing evenly.

MY SECRET-WEAPON BURGER SAUCE

For me, there are three essential components that make a great burger. The best-quality meat you can find, a beautiful, golden, toasted bun, and a next-level, change-your-life-delicious burger sauce. Everything else is bonus. Every great burger place has its own version of "secret sauce"—the sauce of your dreams that takes a burger from drab to fab—and this is mine. Made with a combination of mayonnaise, ketchup, and Dijon mustard, and then amped up with caramelized onions, sweet paprika, and pickles, this sauce is meant to be slathered liberally.

MAKES ABOUT 2 CUPS

2 tablespoons unsalted butter

2 medium white onions, diced

Sea salt

2 garlic cloves, minced

¾ cup mayonnaise, homemade (page 118) or store-bought

½ cup ketchup

2 teaspoons Dijon mustard

1 tablespoon Worcestershire sauce

¼ teaspoon sweet paprika

2 dill pickles, finely chopped

⅓ cup finely sliced fresh chives

1 tablespoon lemon zest

Freshly ground black pepper

In a medium saucepan over medium-low heat, melt the butter. When the butter has melted, add the onions, season with a pinch of salt, and cook, stirring often, until golden and caramelized, 40 to 45 minutes. Add the garlic and cook, stirring, until fragrant, 1 minute more. Remove from the heat.

In a medium bowl, combine the mayonnaise, ketchup, mustard, and Worcestershire sauce and mix well. Add the onions (with any remaining butter from the skillet), paprika, pickles, chives, and lemon zest, and mix well. Season to taste with salt and a few cracks of pepper. Store the sauce in an airtight container in the refrigerator for up to 2 weeks.

Steak Frites with Creamy Whiskey Peppercorn Sauce

3 pounds russet potatoes, scrubbed but not peeled

Peanut oil, for frying

Two bone-in rib eye steaks, each about 1½ inches thick, at room temperature

1 tablespoon extra-virgin olive oil

Sea salt and freshly ground black pepper

2 tablespoons unsalted butter

2 garlic cloves

2 thyme sprigs

2 rosemary sprigs

For the sauce

1 tablespoon black peppercorns

4 tablespoons unsalted butter, divided

2 shallots, peeled and diced

4 garlic cloves, minced

Sea salt

¼ cup your favorite whiskey

⅓ cup heavy (35%) cream

⅓ cup chicken (page 200) or porcini (page 109) stock, homemade or store-bought

2 teaspoons lemon zest

Paris is one of my favorite places on earth (most obvious statement of the century). The City of Love has been a culinary and artistic North Star for as long as I can remember. My move? When I land at Charles de Gaulle airport, I dust off the transatlantic cobwebs and immediately head to a bistro with one goal—find steak frites. A perfectly rustic Parisian bistro, my favorite classic French dish, and a glass or two of cabernet, and I am in my happy place.

This bistro classic is one you should commit to memory, because it's a serious flex to be able to make at home—something most people only associate with restaurants. The real challenge of this recipe lies in the timing, and for that reason this might be a recipe you make with a buddy—one of you can focus on the meat and sauce, while the other works the fry station. And if you're cooking alone and homemade fries feel like too large of an undertaking, you can serve the steak with mashed potatoes or a big salad instead. For a delicious twist, add **2 teaspoons of togarashi spice to the whiskey sauce (trust me).**

Cut the potatoes into ¼-inch-thick batons and place in a large bowl of cold water. Refrigerate for 1 hour. Line a large baking sheet with paper towel and set a wire rack on top.

In a large Dutch oven or high-sided, heavy-bottomed pot, pour the peanut oil to a depth of 3 inches. Heat over medium heat until it reaches 325°F on a deep-frying thermometer. Drain the potatoes and pat completely dry with paper towel.

Working in batches, fry the potatoes for 5 to 6 minutes, turning them every minute or so. The fries will be lightly colored at this point. Transfer the partially cooked fries to the wire rack while you carry on frying the remaining batches; do not discard the oil (you'll need it again later). Let rest on the wire rack while you make your steak.

Heat a 12-inch cast-iron skillet over medium-high heat and get it as hot as the sun. Open any kitchen windows and turn on your hood fan (trust me).

Brush all sides of each steak with olive oil and season well with salt and pepper. Remember, you can't season the inside of the steak, so go extra generous on the outside.

Place your steaks in the skillet and immediately set a timer. Every minute on the minute, flip the steaks. At the 7-minute mark, add the butter, garlic, thyme, and rosemary to the skillet. Continue cooking, constantly basting the steaks with garlicky herb butter, and flipping every minute, until a digital thermometer inserted in the thickest part of the steaks reaches 130°F (perfect for medium-rare, as the internal temperature of the steaks will continue increasing as they rest). Transfer to a cutting board and let rest at least 7 minutes.

recipe continues

While your steak rests, finish frying your fries and make your whiskey peppercorn sauce.

Heat the oil until it reaches 375°F on a deep-frying thermometer. Working in batches, cook the fries again for 2 to 4 minutes, until golden brown and crispy. Drain on the wire rack, and generously season with salt. Let the oil return to 375°F before each batch.

Make the Sauce: Heat the peppercorns in a medium skillet over medium-high heat and toast for 2 minutes. Add 2 tablespoons of the butter, shallots, garlic, and a pinch of salt, and cook, stirring often, until the shallots are softened, 3 to 4 minutes. Remove the skillet from the heat and add the whiskey. Return the skillet to the heat and allow flame to burn off the alcohol, about 1 minute (you can use your trusty barbecue lighter to light a flame here—just be very careful, please). Add the cream, stock, any juices that have come out of the resting steaks, and lemon zest and bring to a boil. Let the sauce cook until thickened, 2 minutes. Remove from the heat, stir in the remaining 2 tablespoons of the butter, and season to taste with salt.

Slice the steaks against the grain into thin slices. Divide among four plates and spoon some of the sauce over. Serve with a pile of fries alongside.

Cooking Note: *This recipe shines when the steak is reverse seared (page 253), taking on a beautiful smoky flavor. Simply smoke for about 1 hour on a pellet grill preheated to 225°F, until the steaks reach an internal temperature of 120°F. Get a skillet ripping hot, then go in with your steaks, and continue cooking per the above instructions, as you would at the 7-minute mark adding butter, garlic, thyme, and rosemary, and cook, flipping every minute on the minute, until your steaks reach an internal temperature of 130°F. Perfect.*

Steak, Mushroom, and Broccoli Rabe Sandwich with Herbed Vinaigrette

For the vinaigrette

1 shallot, roughly chopped

1 garlic clove, roughly chopped

1 cup packed fresh basil

1 cup fresh flat-leaf parsley

Zest of 1 lemon

Juice of ½ lemon

1 tablespoon Champagne vinegar

½ cup extra-virgin olive oil

Sea salt and freshly ground black pepper

For the sandwiches

2 teaspoons unsalted butter, plus more (softened) for buttering the buns

2 teaspoons extra-virgin olive oil

1½ cups sliced cremini mushrooms

½ medium yellow onion, thinly sliced

Sea salt

1 garlic clove, minced

1½ pounds boneless beef rib eye steak, very thinly sliced (see Cooking Note)

½ large bunch broccoli rabe (about ½ pound), chopped into 1-inch pieces

Freshly ground black pepper

4 hoagie (sub) rolls

Over the past few years, I've had the blessing to eat in some of the finest restaurants in the world. Stars from the tire company, white tablecloths, and wine lists from Moncton to Paris. And of course, the food is delicious, and inspiring, and the art behind each dish almost leaves you at a loss for words. Almost. With all of those experiences, though, I continue to return to those dishes that remind me of being a kid, being with loved ones, and having the best time ever while gathered at the communal table. Steak sandwiches, for me, will always be seasoned with nostalgia and one of my favorite dishes on earth.

In my recipe, the thinly sliced meat is quickly pan-fried in a cast-iron skillet set on the grill, which allows you to multitask and toast the buns alongside (though it could also be done on the stovetop if you don't have a grill). The flavor-packed combination of mushrooms, onions, and broccoli rabe tops each sandwich, and a generous drizzle of herby vinaigrette ties it all together. I call for boneless rib eye steak, but you could substitute NY strip or skirt steak. While I don't typically add cheese to this sandwich, you certainly could—try a nice melting cheese like mozzarella or fontina. Long live the king of sandwiches.

Preheat a grill for direct, high-heat grilling (see Notes on Grilling, page 187) and place a large cast-iron skillet on the grill grate to preheat for 15 to 20 minutes. This can, of course, be done on a stovetop, but I absolutely love the smoky deliciousness and depth of flavor that cooking on a grill gives you.

Make the Vinaigrette: In a blender, place the shallot, garlic, basil, parsley, lemon zest, lemon juice, vinegar, and olive oil, and blend until smooth and emulsified. Season to taste with salt and pepper. The vinaigrette can be made up to a day ahead. Refrigerate in an airtight container until ready to use.

Make the Sandwiches: Add the butter and olive oil to the preheated skillet. When the butter has melted, add in the mushrooms and onion, season with salt, and cook, stirring occasionally, until the onions are translucent and beginning to brown, about 10 minutes.

Stir in the garlic and cook for 30 seconds. Add the steak and broccoli rabe, and season with a pinch each of salt and pepper. Cook for 4 to 5 minutes, stirring often, for a juicy and slightly charred medium-rare doneness (cook longer if you prefer your steak more well done).

While the steak is cooking, brush your buns with olive oil or melted butter and toast on the grill grate alongside the skillet of steak until golden brown.

Divide the steak mixture between the toasted buns, spoon some of the vinaigrette over each sandwich, and serve.

Cooking Note: To make slicing the meat thinly a bit easier, freeze the steak for 15 minutes before cutting.

Steak and Shiitake Soba Noodles

8 ounces soba noodles

¼ cup soy sauce

¼ cup freshly squeezed lime juice

1 tablespoon honey

2 garlic cloves, minced

½ tablespoon finely grated fresh ginger

1 teaspoon sesame oil

2 tablespoons grapeseed oil or other neutral oil, divided

6 ounces shiitake mushrooms, trimmed, stemmed, and sliced

Sea salt

1 pound boneless sirloin steak, at room temperature

Freshly ground black pepper

8 ounces baby bok choy, halved

1 cup julienned carrots

3 green onions, thinly sliced

1 cup fresh cilantro

Lime wedges, for serving

Soba noodles, which are made from buckwheat, have a wonderful nutty flavor and toothsome texture. I love the combination of cooked and fresh vegetables in this noodle salad, and the strips of steak make it especially hearty. If you want to keep it vegetarian, however, you could swap the Togarashi Tofu (page 114) for the meat. This is also a great way to use up leftover cooked steak, should you happen to be blessed with some.

Bring a large pot of water to a boil and add the noodles. Cook the noodles according to package instructions, and then immediately rinse them under cold running water. Drain well and transfer to a large serving bowl.

In a medium bowl, whisk together the soy sauce, lime juice, honey, garlic, ginger, and sesame oil.

Heat 1 tablespoon of the grapeseed oil in a large skillet over medium heat until the oil is shimmering. Carefully add the mushrooms and season with salt. Cook until golden brown and starting to crisp, 8 to 10 minutes. Remove from the skillet with a slotted spoon.

Season the steak with salt and pepper, coating all sides. Increase the heat to medium-high and get the skillet rocking hot (open a window and turn on the oven hood). Add the steak and cook for 3 to 4 minutes per side for a medium-rare cooked steak (cook longer if you prefer your steak more well done). Remove from the skillet and let rest for at least 5 minutes before slicing against the grain into thin strips.

While the steak rests, reduce the heat to medium, and add the bok choy. Season with salt and pepper, and cook until the bok choy begins to brown and char, 2 to 3 minutes.

Pour the dressing over the noodles and add the carrots, green onions, mushrooms, and bok choy and toss well to combine. Divide among individual serving plates and top each serving with sliced steak. Garnish with cilantro and serve with lime wedges alongside.

Reverse-Seared Bistecca alla Fiorentina

2 porterhouse steaks
(about 2 to 2½ pounds each
and 2 to 2½ inches thick)

2 fresh rosemary sprigs

2 fresh thyme sprigs

2 tablespoons extra-virgin
olive oil

Sea salt and freshly ground
black pepper

¼ cup melted unsalted butter,
warm

Fleur de sel, for finishing

This is absolutely a special occasion meal, but it's my all-time favorite way to prepare steak. When I cook it, it brings back beautiful memories of trips to Florence, where I've been fortunate enough to spend some time cooking, wine tasting, eating, and just simply living "La Bella Vita." This recipe is inspired by Dario Cecchini, the (in)famous Dante-quoting butcher of the hill town of Panzano, whose signature bistecca, made using Flintstone-size porterhouse steaks, is otherworldly.

In Tuscany, the beef comes from the giant white Chianina beef you see roaming the hillsides. That's part of what makes the dish so special—the meat itself is top quality—but the cooking method also plays a role. Rather than searing the steak in a hot skillet and letting it cook until the meat reaches the desired internal temperature, it is instead cooked low and slow for a long time, just until the internal temperature reaches 120°F, and then seared at the end to brown the exterior. The result is a piece of meat that is cooked perfectly from edge-to-edge (no overcooked exterior and too-rare interior). For this method to work well, however, you have to buy a properly thick steak, at least 2 inches thick. My reverse-searing method works in many applications, but for best results I love to use a pellet grill; those wood pellets add a beautifully smoky depth of flavor that is unforgettable. And though it probably doesn't need to be said, you should splurge on the best-quality meat you can afford. Serve the steak with simple accompaniments—roasted local vegetables or stewed white beans (see the recipes that follow), good wine, and a tableful of your best friends.

Remove your steak from the refrigerator 2 hours before cooking to let the beef come to room temperature. Essential step, friends. You always want to ensure when grilling steak that you let it come to room temperature to help guarantee temperature control throughout the cooking process.

Preheat a grill to 225°F. If your grill has a super smoke option like mine, crank that on. We want to infuse the steak with maximum smoke factor. With a bit of kitchen twine, tie the rosemary and thyme sprigs together, making a little herby bundle of happiness.

Pat the steaks dry with paper towel, and coat in a thin layer of olive oil. Generously season the steaks all over with salt and pepper (go heavy on the seasoning here, y'all). Insert a meat probe into the thickest part of one steak, making sure to avoid the bone or any large pockets of fat. Place directly on the grill grates and cook, lid closed, until the steaks reach an internal temperature of 120°F, about 45 minutes to 1 hour. As always, it's really all about temperature here. Just be sure to keep a close eye on that meat probe. Remove the steaks from the grill, increase the grill temperature to high, and get it blazing hot.

recipe continues

Reinsert the meat probe into one of the steaks and place the steaks back on the grill. Using your herb bundle as a baster, baste the butter all over the top of each steak and close the lid. Sear, flipping halfway through and repeating the basting process, until the steaks reach an internal temperature to 125°F to 130°F for medium-rare steaks (cook a tad longer if you prefer your steak more well done).

Remove from the grill and rest for at least 10 minutes before slicing against the grain into ½-inch-thick slices. Pour any steak juices over the sliced steak and top with a sprinkle of finishing salt.

Harvest Vegetables

SERVES 6 TO 8

1 large acorn squash (1½ to 2 pounds), seeded and cut into ½-inch-thick half-moons

1 pound Brussels sprouts, ends trimmed and halved

1 pound rainbow carrots, peeled

1 pound parsnips, peeled and chopped

1 large red onion, peeled and sliced into half-moons

4 garlic cloves, minced

2 tablespoons chopped fresh rosemary

2 tablespoons chopped fresh sage

1 tablespoon chopped fresh thyme

¼ cup extra-virgin olive oil

2 tablespoons pure maple syrup

Sea salt and freshly ground black pepper

Preheat the oven (or grill) to 400°F and line 2 baking sheets with parchment paper.

In a large bowl, combine the squash, sprouts, carrots, parsnips, onions, garlic, rosemary, sage, and thyme. Toss with the olive oil and syrup, and season with salt and pepper. Divide the vegetables between the prepared baking sheets, arranging them in an even layer. Roast, stirring halfway through, for about 30 to 40 minutes, or until tender and beautifully caramelized.

Cool any leftover vegetables to room temperature, and store in an airtight container in the refrigerator for up to 3 days.

Tuscan-Style White Beans

1 pound dried cannellini beans

10 cups water

3 fresh sage sprigs plus ½ cup sage leaves

1 bay leaf

1 head garlic plus 2 garlic cloves, minced

2 tablespoons extra-virgin olive oil, plus more for drizzling

½ pound bacon, diced

½ teaspoon crushed red pepper flakes

2 medium leeks, white and light green parts only, thinly sliced

Sea salt

1 tablespoon freshly squeezed lemon juice

½ cup finely grated Parmesan cheese

Freshly ground black pepper

The night before cooking, place the beans in a large bowl and cover with at least 2 inches of cold water. Cover and let stand overnight (at least 5 hours, but 8 to 10 hours is best).

The next day, drain the beans, rinse them well, and transfer to a large Dutch oven or stockpot. Add the water, sage sprigs, bay leaf, and head of garlic to the pot. Bring to a boil, lower the heat to medium-low, and let the beans simmer away, uncovered, until tender, about 45 minutes. Drain the beans, reserving at least 1 cup of the cooking liquid (you can reserve the remaining cooking liquid for soup), and discard the sage sprigs, bay leaf, and garlic. Wipe the Dutch oven dry with paper towel.

Line 2 plates with paper towels and set nearby. Return the Dutch oven to the stove over medium heat and add the olive oil. When the oil is shimmering, carefully add the bacon and cook until golden and crispy. Remove with a slotted spoon and transfer to one of the prepared plates. Add the sage leaves to the bacon fat in the Dutch oven and cook until crispy, about 1 to 2 minutes. Remove with a slotted spoon and transfer them to the second prepared plate. Add the 2 cloves of minced garlic and red pepper flakes and cook for 30 seconds, keeping a close watch so they don't burn. Add the leeks, season with a pinch of salt, and cook until softened, about 10 to 12 minutes.

Stir the beans and the reserved cooking liquid into the leek mixture, and season with a pinch or two of salt. Bring to a simmer and cook for 6 to 8 minutes, stirring often, until creamy. Add the crispy bacon, lemon juice, and Parmesan and season the beans to taste with salt and pepper.

Transfer to a serving bowl, drizzle with several glugs of olive oil (go heavy here), and garnish with the crispy sage leaves.

Cool any leftover beans to room temperature, and store in an airtight container in the refrigerator for up to 3 days.

255

Massaman Beef Curry

Massaman curry is the height of soul-warming goodness. This robust braise gets a big punch of flavor from a homemade curry paste, and then another layer of complexity from the fragrant whole spices and aromatics that are added to the braise, including cardamom, cinnamon, and star anise, as well as lemongrass. The coconut milk adds luxurious richness, and the fish sauce gives the braise umami and depth. Cooked slow and low, this braise can (and should) be made on your pellet grill, if you have one, for an extra level of smoky complexity. If you don't have access to one, this dish can definitely be made in your oven as well. Serve this curry with lots of jasmine rice for soaking up the sauce.

Preheat the oven to 350°F.

Make the Curry Paste: In a food processor, combine the peanuts, coconut milk, garlic, ginger, lemongrass, chili, coriander, shrimp paste, brown sugar, cumin, nutmeg, cloves, and cardamom, and pulse until smooth. Measure out 3 tablespoons of the curry paste and set aside; the remaining curry paste can be stored in a jar in the refrigerator for up to 2 weeks.

Make the Curry: Heat the grapeseed oil in a large Dutch oven or high-sided, oven-safe pot over medium heat until the oil is shimmering. Carefully add the beef and brown on all sides, 3 to 4 minutes. Using a slotted spoon, transfer to a plate and set aside. Add the cardamom pods, cinnamon, and star anise, and cook for 45 seconds, until fragrant. Add the onion, cilantro stems, and garlic, season with a pinch of salt, and cook until softened and translucent, about 5 to 6 minutes. Stir in the reserved 3 tablespoons of curry paste and cook, stirring, for 1 minute. Pour in 1 cup of the coconut milk, the stock, and the fish sauce, and add the lemongrass. Bring to a simmer, transfer to the oven or grill, and cook for 1 hour.

After 1 hour, pour in the remaining coconut milk, and then add the potatoes, brown sugar, and tamarind. Return to the oven and cook for another hour, or until the beef and potatoes are fork-tender. Remove and discard the star anise, cinnamon sticks, and lemongrass.

Season to taste with salt, and stir in the peanuts. Top with the fresh basil, and if you like it spicy, sliced red chilies. Serve with jasmine rice. Any leftover curry can be cooled to room temperature, transferred to a lidded container, and stored in the refrigerator for up to 3 days.

For the curry paste

¼ cup roasted unsalted peanuts

2 tablespoons full-fat coconut milk

2 tablespoons fish sauce

5 garlic cloves, roughly chopped

2-inch piece fresh ginger, peeled and roughly chopped

1 stalk lemongrass, trimmed to lower 5 inches, dry outer layers discarded, thinly sliced

1 bird's eye or Thai chili

1 teaspoon ground coriander

1 teaspoon shrimp paste

1 teaspoon dark brown sugar

1 teaspoon ground cumin

⅛ teaspoon nutmeg

⅛ teaspoon ground cloves

¼ teaspoon ground cardamom

For the curry

2 tablespoons grapeseed oil or other neutral oil

2 pounds beef chuck roast, cut into 1-inch pieces

10 cardamom pods, crushed

2 whole cinnamon sticks

3 whole star anise

1 large yellow onion, diced

2 tablespoons finely diced chopped fresh cilantro stems

Sea salt

2 garlic cloves, minced

2 cans (each 14 ounces) coconut milk

1 cup beef stock

2 tablespoons fish sauce

1 lemongrass stalk, halved

1½ pounds baby potatoes, scrubbed

2 tablespoons dark brown sugar

1½ teaspoons seedless tamarind paste

¼ cup unsalted roasted peanuts

Handful of fresh Thai basil

1 to 2 bird's eye or Thai chilies, thinly sliced (optional)

Steamed jasmine rice, for serving

Braised Short Ribs with Colcannon Cakes

For the short ribs

4 tablespoons grapeseed oil or other neutral oil, divided

4 pounds beef short ribs

Sea salt and freshly ground black pepper

1 large yellow onion, diced

2 carrots, peeled and diced

2 celery stalks, diced

2 tablespoons tomato paste

6 garlic cloves, minced

1 bay leaf

2 tablespoons chopped fresh thyme

2 tablespoons fresh rosemary

2 cups (16 ounces) your favorite stout beer

2 cups beef stock

¼ cup chopped fresh flat-leaf parsley

For the colcannon cakes

2½ pounds russet potatoes, peeled

5 tablespoons unsalted butter

3 cups shredded green cabbage

Sea salt

1 cup heavy (35%) cream

3 green onions, sliced

1 cup all-purpose flour

1 large egg, lightly beaten

¼ cup grapeseed oil or other neutral oil

Braising is a perfect technique for cold-weather comfort cooking. Cooked low and slow, tough cuts of meat become tender, the gentle heat breaking down the connective tissue, rendering the meat silky and soft. Short ribs are an incredibly flavorful cut that take a little extra time, love, and tenderness, making them especially well-suited to braising. I use a nice stout beer for a portion of the braising liquid, which gives the sauce incredible body and flavor. Choose one you like to drink—you only need 16 ounces for the recipe, but it's nice to serve some alongside. The colcannon cakes, inspired by a traditional Irish potato and cabbage dish, are just one serving suggestion—the short ribs are also wonderful served with polenta (page 175), garlic mashed potatoes (page 67), or tossed with buttered noodles. A bright and fresh green salad alongside rounds out the meal. Any leftover meat can be shredded and added to tomato sauce (page 92) and served with pasta.

Preheat the oven to 375°F.

Prepare the Short Ribs: Heat 2 tablespoons of the grapeseed oil in a large Dutch oven or high-sided, oven-safe pot over medium heat. Season the short ribs all over with salt and pepper. Working in batches, brown the short ribs, turning, until golden brown all over, about 8 minutes, and then transfer to a rimmed baking sheet.

Add the onion, carrot, celery, and a pinch of salt. Cook, stirring occasionally, until the vegetables are softened and translucent. Add the tomato paste, garlic, bay leaf, thyme, and rosemary and cook, stirring constantly, for 2 minutes. Pour in the stout and stock, season with a pinch each of salt and pepper, and bring to a simmer. Return the short ribs to the pot, transfer to the preheated oven, and braise, uncovered, for 2½ to 3 hours, or until the meat is falling off the bone and your kitchen smells absolutely incredible.

Make the Colcannon Cakes: While the short ribs braise, put the potatoes in a large saucepan and add water to cover by a few inches. Generously salt the water, bring to a boil over high heat, and boil until fork-tender, about 15 to 20 minutes. Drain and transfer to a large bowl.

While the potatoes are boiling, melt the butter in a large skillet over medium heat. Add the cabbage, season with a pinch of salt, and cook for 4 to 5 minutes, until softened and wilted. Add the cabbage to the bowl with the potatoes, along with the cream. Using a potato masher, mash until combined. Fold in the green onions, and season to taste with salt. Add the flour and egg, mix to combine, and form and shape into 1-inch-thick cakes.

Heat the grapeseed oil in a large skillet over medium heat. Working in batches, fry the cakes, turning once, until golden, about 3 to 4 minutes per side.

To serve, transfer the short ribs to a platter and sprinkle with parsley. Serve the colcannon cakes alongside.

Acknowledgments

Thank you. Thank you. Thank you.

Thank you to my forever inspiring, encouraging, supportive, and constantly hungry friends and family. This book exists thanks to my community, for whom I will be forever grateful. Community is everything. Food is community.

A massive thank you to all the chefs, cooks, and food-obsessed folks that I've had the privilege to cook alongside, learn from, and experience unique and life-changing flavors with over the past few years. Each and every time you have the joy to cook or dine with someone, you learn and you grow. I'm the cook I am today thanks to the folks that I've had the privilege to learn from.

Thank you to the farmers, fishermen, producers, and providers; the folks who work tirelessly (and often thanklessly) to ensure we have access to the ingredients we need to create deliciousness. Chefs and cooks cannot do what we do without you. You're the true heroes of the food industry.

Jessica Battilana—the best writing partner a person could ask for! This book wouldn't have happened without you. You're a force. A rockstar. Beyond thankful for your wisdom, guidance, and fervor for deliciousness.

Al Douglas—my photographic partner in crime. Thanks for capturing beautiful moments of community at the table. Grateful to share the stage with you.

To the Harper Celebrate team—Michael Aulisio, Danielle Peterson, Marilyn Jansen, Robin Richardson, and MacKenzie Collier, you're amazing! Thanks for believing in me, this cookbook, and helping so many more folks cook with confidence!!

Maximilian Ulanoff—how the universe decided that the greatest agent on planet earth would also become one of my best friends will remain a mystery for which I'm eternally thankful. Grateful for you, what we've done, and will continue to do.

The incomparable Sarah Passick Baldinger, Mia Vitale, Celeste Fine, and the folks at Park & Fine Literary and Media.

Mom and Dad—I love you. Thanks for your limitless support, love, and counsel. Josh and Katie Prescott, and my beautiful nieces and nephews Ella, Emerson, Lennon, Maisie, and Annie.

Our crack seafood boil extravaganza photoshoot team: Zach Dallaire, Scott Killen, Carole Goguen, Brodye and Rachel Chappel, Jenessa Duval and Maxime Daigle (The Oyster Lord), Natalie LeBlanc Melanson (my heart), and Sage (the goodest lil Mini Golden Doodle).

261

My incredible Traeger Grills family: Jeremy Andrus, Alisha Draney, Hjalmar Hedman, Amanda Schaefer, Nichole Dailey, Krista Bava, Austen Granger, Alex Noshirvan, Luke Edgar, and so many more Wood-Fired rockstars. Team Traeger forever.

Thanks to Bluehouse Salmon, the team at Canon Canada, Hedley & Bennett, World Vision Canada, Guinness, Meater, Eda Kalkay, Lauren Hochhauser, Jamie Youngentob, Mark Moore and the folks at Red Lama Media, Peter McKinnon, Paul Newnham and Chef's Manifesto, Nick Liberato, Karin Bohn, and the entire *Restaurants on the Edge* crew, Broadfork Farm, Netflix, New Brunswick Deliciously Canadian and The Province of New Brunswick, The Cook's Edge, Tosho Knife Arts, Moncton Fish Market, Marché Dieppe, Melody Hillman Ceramics, MMclay, *Food & Wine*, WFP World Food Programme, Epoch Chemistry, Moncton, Riverview, Dieppe, and the countless folks and friends (FAR too many to name) all over the globe who've inspired, encouraged, recipe tested, and supported me over the years. Forever grateful for you. Forever grateful for this beautiful life. Forever thankful for the opportunity to share these stories of food, community, and the power of eating together. Thank you.

Index